'Tis a Gift to be Simple

'Tis a Gift to be Simple

Embracing the Freedom
of Living with Less

Barbara DeGrote-Sorensen
and David Allen Sorensen

Augsburg
MINNEAPOLIS

'TIS A GIFT TO BE SIMPLE
Embracing the Freedom of Living with Less

Scripture quotations unless otherwise noted are from the Holy Bible: New International Version. Copyright 1978 by the New York International Bible Society. Used by permission of Zondervan Bible Publishers.

Adapted text of "Into My Heart" by Harry D. Clarke copyright © 1924, 1952 by Hope Publishing Co., Carol Stream, IL 60188. All rights reserved. Used by permission.

Cover design: Catherine Reishus McLaughlin
Interior design: James Brisson

Library of Congress Cataloging-in-Publication Data

DeGrote-Sorensen, Barbara, 1954–
    'Tis a gift to be simple : embracing the freedom of living with less / Barbara DeGrote-Sorensen and David Allen Sorensen.
      p.   cm.
    Includes bibliographical references.
    ISBN 0-8066-2573-2 (alk. paper)
    1. Christian life—1960– 2. Simplicity—Religious aspects—Christianity. 3. Church and social problems.   I. Sorensen, David Allen, 1953– .   II. Title.   III. Title: It is a gift to be simple.
BV4501.2.D432   1992
241'.68—dc20   92-4181
                                                  CIP

The paper used in this publication meets the minimum requirements of American National Standard for Information Sciences—Permanence of Paper for Printed Library Materials, ANSI Z329.48-1984. ∞™

Manufactured in the U.S.A.   AF 9-2573

96   95   94   93   92   1   2   3   4   5   6   7   8   9   10

*For all those
who are stirred to live simply
that others may simply live.*

CONTENTS

PREFACE

Beware of Bible studies. They may change your life.

This book and the story it tells directly result from eight weeks of studying 1 and 2 Samuel and related Scriptures. We never intended that particular Bible study to send us down a more simple path, but it did. We're still rather surprised. And—in most ways—we couldn't be more pleased.

This is our story. It's worth sharing only because it lets others see the possibility of living life in a way that allows others to live also. We've taken some chances in telling this story. It's not an easy thing to share one's brokenness with others. We've tried to be honest. We still have lots of questions about life-style and its effect on the larger world. Some days we wonder what we've actually accomplished. Some days we fail. Most days, we just breathe more deeply and smile.

Ultimately, simplicity is not something we choose. Rather simplicity chooses us. Once convicted, there is no choice in the matter. It simply has to be done. That knowledge replaces the fear of change with a quiet joy. This is right and good. Kind. Gentle.

Being convicted by simplicity means that we stop to honestly evaluate our priorities and apply ourselves to integrating these priorities into the way we live. Simplicity requires us to change not only how we live but also how we think and how we view the world and the people around us.

Simplicity is more than time management. It's more than wholistic health. It's more than quality time versus quantity time, self-care versus social reform. Simplicity requires us to become more focused—to serve one God instead of many.

Simplicity coaxes change in the core of our being as we begin to question some widely held assumptions and ask ourselves:

- What are the values that guide my actions?
- What is my fair share?
- When is enough enough?
- Why don't I feel good?
- How can I live a more integrated faith?
- Who are my neighbors, and do I really care about them?

For those who have felt gentle nudges toward a less hectic life, this book is a primer for getting their lives, possessions, attitudes, priorities, and actions back in rhythm with the one who created them.

This is also a book with no ending. That is the way it should be. Simplicity is an ongoing process, a joyful experience of detaching ourselves from what is less important and attaching ourselves to that which is more important. Each of us has the opportunity to write our own chapter in this never-ending story. We invite you to try. Embrace the magnificent conspiracy called simplicity and all its gifts. It will change your life.

We are grateful that God continues to communicate to us through the Scriptures. We pray that God will speak to you, calling us all to a life lived out in the awareness of others.

Blessings on your journey.

Barbara DeGrote-Sorensen
David Allen Sorensen

CHAPTER 1

If I Could Put Time in a Bottle

To everything there is a season and a time . . .

ECCLESIASTES 3:1

It was a typical Bible study. Eight adults, their chairs in a circle, all looking to glean a special kernel of truth from the morning's lesson.

The story was familiar. We read from Luke 7 about a woman who lived a sinful life, wet Jesus' feet with her tears, wiped them with her hair, and poured perfume on them. It was an old custom to welcome weary travelers played out in a dramatic way, but what could it possibly say to eight women of today, most of whom had short hair and a half-dozen partially used perfume bottles at home?

"What expensive gift might we pour on Jesus' feet today?" the leader asked.

I looked around the group. No one had a quick answer. The perfume was extravagant because the woman did not have a lot of it. It cost her something to use the perfume—to literally pour it out—because it was limited. One jar.

"Anybody have an idea?" the leader prodded. "What is an extravagant gift today? What could we give that would cost us something?"

One weary voice spoke for the group. "Time," she said.

1

We all nodded in agreement. To pour out one's time was indeed an extravagant gift. Although most of us had more than enough possessions to meet our needs, nobody ever seemed to have enough time.

Time. I thought about that answer all the way home and shared it with David that night before he drove off to get the sitter and we both ran off to meetings. What were we doing with our time? Why were we always so tired—so rushed? Why did what we own never seem enough? What were we missing along the way?

Addicted to our own adrenaline, we sprinted from one meeting to the next, one more appointment, one more deadline, saying, "If we can just hang on until things slow down, maybe in March, or April. . . ." But March and April had their own expectations, and we always postponed that break in the action a few more weeks. Always a few more weeks. Always hanging in there until next time.

We weren't alone. Many of us move from one house to another, one job to another, always on our way up. We consume our own energy resources faster than we can replenish them, making ourselves sick in the process and call the whole thing good. What an insane way to live. What a common way to live.

Something is out of whack, out of sync with that "still, small voice" that keeps calling us to calm down and be quiet in the presence of God. After a while our crazy pace isn't fun anymore. What we need is a stop sign to pull us up short. For me it took a big truck.

Backing into a Beginning

I remember the morning well. I was on my way to the clinic at 6:45 A.M. for blood tests. It was the last part of a

checkup my doctor had suggested to make sure my headaches weren't anything serious. As I sped down the highway,
my thoughts were on the long list of things waiting for my
attention that day. Too much. Always too much. I could
never get it all done. Job, family, church. Forget friends or
fun. Those were the real luxuries.

The stop sign at the end of the hill forced me to stop
and pause. I hated this intersection. Four lanes of traffic to
cross with a lane in the middle for left turns. I decided to
pull out halfway and wait until the farther lanes cleared
before trying to merge. I looked at my watch. I had seven
minutes to go across town and catch the main artery now
swelling with early morning traffic. By my calculations I
would be four minutes late. My head started to pound as
I geared up and headed into the intersection.

It was a busy morning. But busy was good. Life didn't
seem to count unless I functioned at a roller coaster pace.
Busyness meant that I counted for something, that I was
being mature, holding up my part, being responsible. All
I had to do was say I was busy and people would nod their
heads knowingly. "How are you? Busy? Good, good." It
was an old conversation.

The horn from a red hatchback stopped my car halfway
across the first two lanes. I glared at the driver who had
left me hanging out in the intersection as she attempted
her left turn. "Move!" I mouthed silently from inside my
own vehicle. Yes, I knew she had the right of way. I had
the stop sign. But I *was* out in the intersection first. Neither
of us was going anywhere.

Aware of approaching cars, I glared again at the young
woman blocking my path. Blood tests were not worth dying

for, I told myself. I angrily put my car in reverse and roared back toward my stop sign. The red hatchback squealed by me as I crashed into a truck that had, unbeknownst to me, approached the intersection.

All I really remember of the next five minutes was an angry guy yelling, "Hey, lady . . ." and an exchange of telephone numbers for insurance purposes.

I sat shaking in the front seat of my car. I could have killed someone. I could have killed myself. As I eased into the traffic, my thoughts and feelings tumbled in slow motion. One of many fender benders in the country that day, this experience became for me a reawakening.

All that running hadn't accomplished anything except to make my life miserable and me not much fun to live with. Rush, rush, rush. Hurry, hurry, hurry. And for what? To be honest, I would have to say, "Because it made me feel important." Important people always rush. Having no time was a status symbol.

I resolved to take that stop sign at face value and stop my insane pace before it stopped me. I began to take a long look at what was important to me, where I was spending my time, and why I never felt well. What I found was that I had trapped myself into a life-style that didn't mirror my true values and priorities. This wind-up-toy life-style demanded I march to its pace. I wanted my life back. I knew it would mean changing something, even some big things, but I was determined to find a different pace for this marathon called life that would leave me with breath at the finish line.

I was convinced. Now to convince the rest of my family.

David's "Beginning"

Barbara began talking about her longing for simplicity first.

"We are living comfortably, not extravagantly," I defended. "Look, we live on a little cul-de-sac that's safe for the kids, and that's important too. All right, it's just off a golf course, and granted, we both have to keep working hard in order to live here, but. . . ."

She didn't push. She just kept coming home from the Bible study with a lot of questions about how we were living. *Are we spending our time in a way that's consistent with what we say is important to us? Are we spending our money in ways that are healthy? What difference does the fact that we are Christians make in our life-style?*

I admit I dragged my feet. Why force change? Changes can be painful.

Looking back, I realize I had fallen for "the American dream." American *heresy* is more like it. Buy now; pay later. Don't keep cars more than two or three years—too much of a hassle. Get as much house as you can beg, steal, or borrow. Mostly borrow.

I remember being introduced to the need for credit cards on our honeymoon. "Any major credit card would do," the manager said as we registered. I didn't have one. She sniffed at me. The hotel wouldn't accept my check, even with proper identification. "Give me a break. It's our honeymoon," I said, humiliated in front of my young bride. "Sorry," the woman replied. I had to go back to the car and open enough wedding cards to pay cash for one night.

I got my first credit card the next week. A dozen years later we had enough credit cards to make my wallet uncomfortable to sit on for long.

In the years before we made some life-style changes we were introduced to the consolidation loan—a loan to pay off other loans. I know it's not a good idea. But we had just bought our first house, and we immediately needed a refrigerator, a mower, a dishwasher, a remodeled kitchen, a new deck. . . . You guessed it. We used the cards.

Two experiences helped change my heart.

I was in the delivery room with Barb following the birth of our son. With two terrific little girls already at home, having a son was a very fine moment. People had been telling us, "Hope you have your boy!" We answered honestly, "We'll be happy either way as long as the baby is healthy." Still, is *was* nice to have a boy.

The nurse checked him, gave him a ten on a ten-point scale—healthy!—then said I should take my child to the nursery while they settled Barb in her room. But later as they examined him further, they found a 1-in-15,000 life-threatening birth defect in the digestive tract. Hours later, Barb and I were pacing the halls at the University of Minnesota Hospital while our precious one had his first surgery. Afterward, the surgeon outlined for us a rather rigorous twice-a-day therapy that would both help him and cause him pain.

Something clicked in me at that moment. Previously, I had been a person who would sell or get rid of something that was on the fritz. But this time it was my son who had trouble! Of course I would do whatever it took to make him better. This incident changed the way I understood the gifts God had given me. It also changed my motivation to care for those gifts.

The other experience that changed my heart was a three-week trip to Tanzania, East Africa. I thought I was prepared for the culture shock. After all, I had lived in Tanzania for two years as a teenager, and I had traveled in some twenty-five countries in the twenty years that followed. But since I had lived there, Tanzania had become the second-poorest country in the world, after Bangladesh. As I traveled in some of the most poverty-stricken, remote parts of that country, seeing how they lived caused me physical pain. Yet the people were gracious and kind. "Are you sure these people are happy?" I repeatedly asked our escort.

"It's all relative," my Masai friend replied. "They have never been to America. They don't even have radios to know how people live in Dar es Salaam. They're happy."

When I came home, I was ready to make some changes. Finally.

Making Changes

After those individual promptings for change, we were each ready for what followed. We didn't begin this journey looking for simplicity. What we wanted was more time. More control of our lives. Simplicity came to us as a gift, a consequence of decisions we made to live at a more even pace.

To gain more time, we needed to change how we spent our time. We began letting go in ways we will explain throughout this book. There is no one way to a more simple life-style. Each person's journey is unique. Our way was to close our eyes and jump. Others who are more patient will take one step at a time. Either way, what we gain is not a new pit of legalism but a newfound understanding of God's grace.

In retrospect I can say it was fun because it was freeing. It changed our lives.

Feet First

Not everybody would have called us "conspicuous consumers." Sure, we lived in a nice neighborhood. High taxes? Yes. Chemlawn? Most people had it. It didn't seem out of line. But it took two incomes for us to stay there, and our charge card statements reminded us monthly that we were losing ground.

Exactly what were our house payments? How much did we owe on credit cards? That's not the point. The fact is, we felt overextended and out of control—in our money, in our time, in our spirits.

Step one was to free ourselves of some of that cumbersome load. We put our house on the market. We reduced our job commitments by half. We cut other things in half: mortgage, taxes, house size. A drastic move? Yes. A bit hasty? Perhaps. But it allowed us the energy to breathe easy once again.

There were withdrawal symptoms. Old habits are hard to break. Old voices continued to scream, "Hurry up! No one moves down. Up is the way to go. Up, up, up. More, more, more." But slowly we gained the needed space to reflect. We played more with our children. We filled the void with good books and conversation. We still had some frantic nights when everyone needed to be somewhere at the same time but far fewer than before. In the quiet moments we began to find value in important things we once labeled a waste of time.

And we found a place for God. Even though we were both employed at a church, our God and our faith had too often become lost in a crowded schedule. Somehow we had forgotten about that relationship that needed nourishing. "I'm doing this for God," we had told ourselves. And we believed it. But in the running we had forgotten that God asks for simple "obedience, not sacrifice." God's voice is still and small. We couldn't hear him over the flurry of activity.

Slowly, we began to reclaim what we had desired in the first place—an integrated faith. One that represented what we believed and also left room for reflection.

There are many ways to "move down." Our beginning step was a drastic one. You can begin in smaller ways; first, by accepting the fact that your life's pace is not what you want it to be and you long for a simpler life. Your very dissatisfaction may, in fact, be the working and prompting of the Holy Spirit. Are you unsure of the source of your longing? Begin to give yourself that needed space to hear once again God's will for you.

A "move down" buys you time, an opportunity to be in a place where God can speak. What we eat, how we live, how long we keep our cars, and how we use credit may sound like a new set of laws—a new sort of legalism. It need not be. Rather, think of it as the riverbanks that guide the flow of water. Without that perspective, simplicity becomes nothing more than another trend—another way to

show who we are by what we don't own, what we don't
wear, what we won't eat, or whether or not we recycle. It's
the same old game, only in reverse.

Let this movement toward simplicity be a way to allow
space for a fuller relationship with God. God is seeking us,
stirring our hearts to seek after him, to seek after a more
meaningful life. But God does not force a way into anyone's
life. Let us take God seriously and make choices which
allow prime time for that relationship.

Society appears to be moving toward wholeness. A more
practical baby boomer generation—growing older and wiser,
having had it all—now desires meaning and purpose. But
if a trend for less does arise out of the emptiness that excessive living has generated, it will be nothing more than
a trend unless it is grounded in something greater than
ourselves.

This book is not intended to support a social trend. It is
intended to give some guidelines for finding a place where
our relationship with God can be nurtured and can grow.
Think of it as a doorway into a new pace for your life—a
chance to step back and hear again that still, small voice
that says, "I have called you by name. You are mine."

CHAPTER 2

Moving Down

Once we accept the realization that the day of automatically increasing wealth are past, a more serene and balanced future awaits us. Our hunger for more, one of our oldest and deepest traits, will have to be nourished by things other than money. Our values will shift so that a sense of purpose and an ethic of service and the desire to make a difference will be afforded a new respect. Perhaps, we'll even learn to be more content with the tremendous wealth and privileges we already have.

LAURENCE SHAMES,
THE HUNGER FOR MORE[1]

We can choose how we live. God created us with the power to choose. Perhaps that is part of what it means to be created in God's image. By choosing well, we can make our lives more manageable and more meaningful.

The following anecdote by an anonymous author was torn from the back of a church newsletter found in our home.

Two friends, Timothy and Christopher, new converts to a little mission church, were having the following discussion:

> *"Christopher, if you had a hundred sheep, would you give fifty of them for the Lord's work?"*

> *"Yes, Timothy, I would."*
>
> *"Would you do the same if you had a hundred cows?"*
>
> *"Yes, I would."*
>
> *"Would you do the same if you had a hundred horses?"*
>
> *"Yes, of course."*
>
> *"If you had two pigs, would you give one of them to the Lord?"*
>
> *"No, I wouldn't; and you have no right to ask me, Timothy, for you know I have two pigs."*

Moving down—purposely living more simply than we once thought possible—is easy to admire in someone else. Everyone would agree that generosity and selflessness are good—a worthy response to Christ's love for us. To work that out practically becomes more difficult.

Jesus told his followers: "Sell your possessions and give to the poor. Provide purses for yourselves that will not wear out, a treasure in heaven that will not be exhausted, where no thief comes near and no moth destroys. For where your treasure is, there your heart will be also" (Luke 12:33-34).

These are not easy Scriptures. Clearly, Christ is asking something of us. Poverty is not the issue here. Generosity is. And this passage is one of many Scriptures in the Old and New Testaments that deals with money and what we do with it. One source found that one verse in six in the Old Testament and one verse in seven in the New Testament addresses the topics of money and possessions. Sixteen of Jesus' parables deal with stewardship of the gifts that God has given us.[2] What are we supposed to do with all these teachings?

Moving down—beginning the process of living less extravagantly than we once thought possible—is called "voluntary simplicity." Voluntary simplicity is a way for us to live, asking only our "fair share" and allowing us to be generous with the rest.

Voluntary simplicity allows us to be a servant church. For most of us, though, there are some real stumbling blocks that keep us from taking this challenge seriously.

Old Arguments

Argument #1—"But I've *earned* it. I've put in my hours."

The concept of tithing—sharing 10 percent of our income with others—comes from the Old Testament. Therefore, some people see it as less binding after the time of Christ. In the early church, as the book of Acts describes, people pooled their resources to meet the needs of many. In New Testament terms none of it is mine. All is a gift. No matter how I have earned my money or acquired my degree of success, everything has been a gift because God first gifted me with the skills necessary to accomplish what I have done. Some of us have made good use of our gifts, and doing so has given us a comfortable life. But the purpose of the gift was not to make us comfortable; it was to make us generous. In this framework, the perspective no longer is "how much do I have to give?" The better point of view says, "Even after giving liberally, look how much I am blessed to keep for myself!"

Argument #2—"I'm only living out my fair share. I can't afford to live more simply than I am."

"Fair share" is a matter of perspective. "Normal" is what we're used to, and as North Americans we are used to plenty. In a world overflowing with people and problems, statistics of poverty and descriptions of third-world conditions often go by us without our even shaking our heads. To jar us out of this desensitized mind-set, it might help to distill the numbers and look at ourselves the way the rest of the world sees us.

Joan Bodner, in her book *Taking Charge of Our Lives— Living Responsibly in a Troubled World*, symbolizes the world and its resources as a small village. She writes:

> *If the world were a global village of 100 people, one-third of them would be rich or of moderate income, two-thirds would be poor. Of the 100 residents, 47 would be unable to read, and only one would have a college education. About 35 would be suffering from hunger and malnutrition, at least half would be homeless or living in sub-standard housing. If the world were a global village of 100 people, 6 of them would be Americans. These 6 would have over a third of the village's entire income, and the other 94 would subsist on the other two-thirds. How could the wealthy 6 live in peace with their neighbors? Surely they would be driven to arm themselves against the other 94—perhaps even to spend, as Americans do, about twice as much per person on military defense as the total income of two-thirds of the villagers.*[3]

Statistics clearly show that North Americans live excessively in relation to the rest of the world. In general, we ignore these statistics because we find it easier to compare ourselves to those who have more rather than those who have less. Comparing ourselves with those who have more makes it easier for us to keep accumulating.

What Does It All Mean?

The purpose of all this is to stop and reconsider what it means to be Christ-followers—to look at what Christ said about how we are to live our faith. How might we respond in an integrated and authentic way to the gift of grace God has given us? How might we be obedient to the one who chose to associate himself with the powerless and poor, the common and the hurting. Doesn't following Christ also mean following his teachings?

Few people would not choose voluntarily to simplify their lives—to intentionally move down—if the need were put on their doorstep. We are still, despite our apparent greediness, a compassionate people when we understand the need.

In the country of Haiti, 20 percent of the children (one in five) die before their fifth birthdays. We could list numerous "causes of death," but the true cause is poverty. Suppose an advocate for that one-in-five child were to ask the United States for a sponsor so that this child might have what is necessary to sustain her life. You know that somewhere, someone would rise to take that challenge. Suppose that one-in-five child came to your town and asked the community to help her give others like herself what they needed in order to grow. The community would stir, contacting churches and civic organizations. After much discussion and many proposals, more than likely those needs would be met. You might read about it in the paper and feel good about what your community did, but you yourself might not feel the need to help.

But suppose that one-in-five child, named Anna, came to your door and knocked. When you opened the door, you saw her standing there with boney legs, distended stomach, and dirty face. You know that you would take her in, call your doctor and other professionals, and do what was needed to sustain her life. When the need is on our doorstep, we are more likely to respond.

If we listen, we can hear that the hungry are knocking. The sick are knocking. The homeless, lonely, and abused are knocking . . . knocking . . . knocking. . . .

What are we to do?

It doesn't seem right that we ignore all the knocking just because it isn't precisely on our own front doors.

Moving down allows us to close the distance between those who have and those who have not, to live with the poor not only on our doorsteps but at our tables. Voluntary simplicity, to purposely choose to live more simply so that others may simply live, is not a cookie-cutter philosophy. Each one of us lives it out in our own circumstances and situations as we accept the grace to do so. Voluntary simplicity does not mean we all have to sell our homes. It doesn't even mean we can't have nice things. It may mean that we can't have all of them.

Like anything else, however, it does require a beginning. Moving down is like putting a pencil to our life's story and asking, "What can I cross out and still have an abundant life? What excess can I remove from my life that will help me express my true values? What parts of my life's story are distractions that only keep me off pace and running ragged?"

Our family's dentist is a kind and gentle man, a Christian who sometimes shares faith stories with his patients as he works on their teeth. Although they are a captive audience, most people don't seem to mind. At our last checkup the conversation went something like this:

"I thought you had moved," he said, surprised to see me.

"No. We just moved across town."

"Needed a bigger house, huh?"

"No, actually we moved down." I rattled off some of our recent discoveries of the joy and freedom in living more simply.

"Open, please. That's interesting. My wife and I did the same thing. We live two blocks over now. I walk to work. We got rid of one of our cars. I just told my wife one day, 'You can't have me and all this, too.' I cut back on hours. I've got more family time now. It's funny. Living more with less. You know what I mean?"

"Uh huh."

"So you made a move down. Funny to find someone else out there doing it, too."

I swallowed and smiled. "Well, good for you."

"Good for you, too."

What began as a way to stop our endless running—to find our pace—soon affected our choices about consumption. As we simplified the internal stimulation that had kept us so wired, we soon found ourselves wanting to simplify the rest of our lives also. It made sense that living at a more peaceful pace would also mean living less affluently. "Living more with less" seemed almost fun as we began taking steps toward finding a pace more in step with world standards of eating, housing, and consumption in general.

Just Think of It

What would happen if you or your family voluntarily chose to cut your own expenses and put those unspent assets toward a common goal? You could start with one thing—one small thing. Less eating out. Another winter on a coat that's only slightly out of date. A used car instead of a new one. People might notice. They might even ask you why. Voluntary simplicity might not change the world, but it will leave a mark. It could be a witness of Jesus Christ's gift of grace in your life.

Voluntary simplicity is not a matter of salvation. It has nothing to do with whether God will love us or not. God loves us whether we respond to him and try to follow his teachings or not. That is the incredible, unconditional love of God.

Voluntary simplicity is not a matter of salvation. It is a matter of obedience—to live a faith integrated with life, to live as Christ taught, to live as Christ lived, joyously aware that we have the ability to be generous if we so choose.

CHAPTER 3

Because I Can

In a world where nearly 1 billion people live near the edge of physical survival the relevance of intentional simplicity by the more affluent people of the world cannot be overestimated.

DUANE ELGIN, *VOLUNTARY SIMPLICITY*[1]

With mixed feelings we signed on the dotted line to close the deal on our newly acquired home. Could five people and a dog fit into 950 square feet and still like each other? Looking over the income stats required to process our loan, our realtor shook his head. "Well, that's it," Lenny said, putting the final stamp on the top paper. "But I still don't get it. Why'd you buy such a small house, anyway?"

We tried without success to explain our desire for a simpler life. Buying beneath one's ability did not make good business sense in Lenny's line of work.

"Not me," he said. "I just got a friend to float me a loan on a three-thousand-plus square footer."

"Do you have a lot of kids?" we asked.

"None yet. Haven't had time."

"Then why'd you buy such a *big* house?"

Lenny looked startled. He wasn't used to being challenged about such an obvious thing. "Well . . . because I can," he answered.

It's the American way to buy as much as we can just *because* we can. No other reason is needed. However, the

heart that seeks simplicity occasionally makes life-style
changes in the *other* direction—just because we can.

Intentional simplicity—voluntary simplicity—means living with less than we are able. It means stepping out of
the swift current of overconsumption and making decisions
based on very different values.

Americans are taught to know what they want, but they
may not have a clear sense of what they need.

The difference between excessive living and sufficient
living is not a hot topic at dinner parties. It's hard to imagine
a television show entitled "Life-styles of the Poor and Humble." Sufficient living is not flashy. It doesn't follow the
rule of looking out for number one.

But who's writing the rules? Who's holding the hoops
we're supposed to jump through? Who's creating this of-
course-you-want-it pace that keeps us moving up, up, up?

Who writes the rules?

One car company uses the slogan, "Oh, what a feeling,"
to sell their product. A competitor places a young blond
behind the wheel, and she heads out over the isolated
morning countryside singing, "Don't want to just drive. I
want to feel good!" The message is clear: "We're not just
selling cars here, folks. We're selling self-esteem."

The message behind the advertisements is that buying
this product will make us like ourselves better. Drug pushers
use the same propaganda for selling drugs: "It'll make you
feel good." You can sell almost anything that promises to
make the buyer feel good.

One can easily draw a parallel between our reasons for overconsumption and a classic fable by Hans Christian Andersen. In the story of "The Emperor's New Clothes" two swindlers sell a vain emperor an invisible suit of clothes. The partners in crime assure him that people who are unworthy for their post or lacking intelligence will not be able to see it. Looking in the mirror, the emperor is horrified that he appears nude. But, not wanting to appear unworthy or unintelligent, he greatly praises the crooked tailors and leads a procession down the main street in view of his subjects.

The local people can clearly see that the emperor is wearing no clothes, but, not wanting to appear unworthy or unintelligent, they, too, ooh and aah over the beauty of the emperor's new clothes. Finally, a child pipes up. "But he's got nothing on." The crowd of people, realizing what is happening, drop their pretense and agree with the child. The emperor, too, finally realizes the truth. But, incredibly, he says, "The procession must go on now." And he continues anyway!

Like the emperor's scoundrel tailors, crass advertising has sold us an "invisible" bill of goods. Living higher than almost any other world citizens, we have been told that those with intelligence, sophistication, and money wear them on their sleeves. At times, all it takes for whole groups of people to see the truth is a small, solitary voice from the crowd. The procession of vanity may continue anyway, but at least some will see it for what it is—a mirage, an image, something that has power only because we give it power.

In our family we have a game we play with our kids when wandering the halls of a store with enticing merchandise.

Any parent knows the tirade of demands children can make when they are overstimulated with so much stuff. The "I want that!" demand in our family has been changed to "I like that!" Our children are allowed to like as much as they want, and they are comfortable with the fact that they don't have to own it to like it. Most of the time, that's enough for them.

Adults can learn the same lesson. Just because we like something doesn't mean we have to own it. We can admire a great many things, but we don't have to add them to the pile of treasures we already possess.

Charge It, Please

For too many people vanity is not the only stumbling block to voluntary simplicity. Too many of us have gotten used to saying, ". . . because I can" when really we can't. Pretend money, in the form of credit cards, has given power—or at least the illusion of power—to advertising agencies who prey on those who "can't wait" and can't say no.

Credit has become for some a new addiction. Our mail regularly brings yet another letter promising preapproved credit. Indebtedness, the old cash advance, instant money, and six-months-free financing have become the norm rather than the sign of shortfall. Debt that appears normal to us would not be understood in many other countries where debt is something to be paid off as quickly as possible—not month by month, paying only the minimum amount required.

One commercial for a shopping center showed a woman loading up her wallet with charge cards much as a cowboy loads his gun with bullets. We're talking power shopping here. It sounds irresistible, and for many it is.

Bankruptcy used to be tragically preceded by a sudden illness or loss of job. Today, many couples with two incomes take that route simply because they have overextended. Bankruptcy has become another viable financial option at the tail end of a run of artificial extravagance.

The "first world" way of life may look good on the surface, but in reality a lot of what is purchased is not owned but borrowed. The truth often is, "All this stuff isn't mine. It belongs to Mastercard, American Express, or the local bank." Before we can begin to practice voluntary simplicity, we first must dig ourselves out from under our debt. It is the first step we can take to reestablish our own financial pace. If we are to practice voluntary simplicity, to live less extravagantly than we are able, we need first to cut the ties of indebtedness that strangle our resource-sharing ability.

A Time for Grieving

I remember how embarrassed I felt the first time friends came over to visit after our move to the smaller house.

I talked too much about why we moved down, stating my intentions too loudly. It's not that we *have* to move down, you see; it's because of these principles.

How noble. The truth was that in slowing our pace, we had made certain life-style decisions. Having set a goal to be out of debt as soon as possible, we knew something had to go. The house seemed the logical choice, but I didn't realize how much of my self-esteem had been wrapped up

in how others perceived me. I didn't want our friends thinking our move down meant that we were in financial diffi-
culties, that we couldn't afford our old life-style anymore.

There is a great feeling of freedom in cutting back our
consumption, but often grieving is part of the process, too.
Embarrassment and low self-esteem may surface when we
begin to rebuild our sense of self not from our possessions
or our power to buy them but from a new set of values that
asks only for our "fair share." "Give me neither poverty nor
riches; feed me with the food that is needful for me" (Prov.
30:8, RSV).

Ten Reasons for Choosing a Simpler Life-style

In light of today's global realities, Jorgen Lissner, secretary for Peace, Justice, and Human Rights in the Lutheran
World Federation, asks comfortable Christians to consider
ten good reasons for reviewing their life-styles:

1. As an *act of faith* performed for the sake of personal
   integrity and as an expression of a personal commitment
   to a more equitable distribution of the world's resources.
2. As an *act of self-defense* against the mind- and body-pol-
   luting effects of over-consumption.
3. As an *act of withdrawal* from the achievement-neurosis
   of our high-pressure, materialistic societies.
4. As an *act of solidarity* with the majority of humankind,
   which has no choice about life-style.
5. As an *act of sharing* with others what has been given to
   us, or of returning what was usurped by us through unjust
   social and economic structures.

6. As an *act of celebration* of the riches found in creativity, spirituality and community with others, rather than in mindless materialism.

7. As an *act of provocation* (ostentatious *under*-consumption) to arouse curiosity leading to dialogue with others about affluence, alienation, poverty, and social injustice.

8. As an *act of anticipation* of the era when the self-confidence and assertiveness of the underprivileged forces new power relationships and new patterns of resource allocation upon us.

9. As an *act of advocacy* of legislated changes in present patterns of production and consumption, in the direction of a new international economic order.

10. As an *exercise of purchasing power* to redirect production away from the satisfaction of artificially created wants, toward the supplying of goods and services that meet genuine social needs.[2]

Lissner follows this list with this insight: "The adoption of a simpler lifestyle is meaningful and justifiable for any or all of the above reasons *alone* regardless of whether it benefits the underprivileged."[3] He has not created a new set of rules; individuals need to develop their own guidelines appropriate for their situation and ability. Simplicity may be adopted for the wrong reasons: guilt, piety, or a "poor me" attitude that says, "If I can't have it, I don't want it." Living simply, in its worst form, can become a sophisticated way to "opt out."

What Lissner has proposed is not a new law but rather an invitation to join the magnificent conspiracy to free ourselves from what ails us.

Voluntary simplicity allows people the opportunity to consume their fair share and be generous with the rest. It is not a cure-all, but it does shake the social, economic, and political structures that blind the affluent to the needs of the rest of the world.

The American dream may say, "You can have it all." But we can say, "I don't buy that" . . . literally. We may not be able to cure poverty, but at least we can live in a way that doesn't laugh in its face. And we can do it gladly—because it is our choice.

"Just because we can!"

CHAPTER 4

Why Don't I Feel Good?

*Don't you know that your body is the temple of the Holy
Spirit, who lives in you, the Spirit given you by God?
You do not belong to yourselves but to God; he bought you
for a price. So use your bodies for God's glory.*

1 CORINTHIANS 6:19-20 (TEV)

Steve is one of those guys everybody likes. Gregarious
and competent, he tackles projects with gusto and enthu-
siasm. Although he works a full-time job, his extra interests
in church and community rarely offer him a night off as he
grabs supper and jumps off to the next meeting. Although
Steve loves his family, family time is rare due to so many
other pressing appointments and expectations.

Recently, Steve's endless energy has waned. Severe
headaches have put him even further behind in his commitments. He has gained weight and knows he should exercise, but he can't seem to set aside time for it. He seems
short tempered with his wife and family and finds himself
making excuses more and more, begging off on commitments. Steve knows he needs to slow down, but he doesn't
like to let people down. "It's all so important . . ." he tells
his wife as he gulps three aspirins and heads for the car.

Joann and Peter were excited about their move up to
their first home. Not wanting to commit two incomes to a
mortgage, they looked at several homes, but all of them

seemed too average. When the realtor told them about a house that had been put back on the market that morning because the prospective buyers hadn't been able to raise the downpayment, Joann and Peter went to look. Although the asking price was more than they wanted to spend, the house had everything they had ever wanted, and it was in a great neighborhood.

They signed the contract that day.

As time wore on, their monthly payments became more and more of a burden. "We never have money for fun anymore," Joann complained as she finished paying bills and closed the checkbook.

They began to rely on their credit cards to bail them out. When neighbors asked Joann and Peter to join them for a weekend away, they were embarrassed to say they didn't have the money, so they charged a cash advance and went anyway. Lately, they have found themselves fighting more often over things that once would have made them laugh.

When Joann found out she was pregnant, they stopped to take a realistic look at where their financial decisions had taken them. Without Joann's job they would be in over their heads. With it they were barely hanging on. Something had to give. They hoped it wasn't their marriage.

Bob is an easygoing guy most of the time. He takes a lot of things for granted—his job, his family, and his health. While others on his block put out their weekly recycling, Bob tosses an aluminum can in the garbage without much thought about where it goes next. He pumps himself up with sugar and caffeine for breakfast. Although he could carpool, he drives alone to work so he can leave when he wants to. "I'm doing OK for me," Bob says. "No one says

Instead it collects on artery walls, choking off the blood supply to our bodies.[5]

It is harder than ever to ignore the mounting research on the effects of stress upon the immune system. Clearly, a healthy life-style—paying attention to diet, exercise, and mental health—contributes to good health overall.[6]

It isn't just unhealthy environments that make us sick. We can get out of pace from internal stimulation as well.

Consider caffeine, a popular villain that continues to cause internal disorder. What happens when we swallow that twelve-ounce can of a caffeinated beverage or down that morning cup of coffee? Our body gets out of pace as a chain reaction of internal events begins.

Caffeine stimulates the release of blood sugar. The pancreas then kicks in with more insulin to reduce the blood sugar, and we begin to feel tired and irritable, or we get a headache.[7] As we rub our head and reach for the aspirin one more time, we ask that old question, "Why don't I feel good?"

Does making a space for God mean a healthy diet, exercise, and good mental health? If we believe this is God's will for us, yes. "Don't you know that your body is the temple of the Holy Spirit, who lives in you, the Spirit given you by God?" (1 Cor. 6:19 TEV).

Are we out of pace with our eating habits? Was our last bit of exercise a walk to the Dairy Queen? Do we find ourselves acting spiritually double-minded—saying we believe one thing about the care of our body and doing another?

Aside from medical reasons, maybe we don't feel good because we are out of relationship with our Creator. According to the Bible, a broken relationship with God is called

"sin," and the consequences of sin include even more brokenness and eventually death.

We're More Than Physical Creatures

Perhaps we need to move for a moment beyond merely
talking about the physical benefits of good diet, exercise,
and time management. Feeling good is not the ultimate
objective; living in a healthy relationship with God is.

With that overarching goal we begin to make choices that
help us stay in a right relationship with God. We can discover
an environment in which worship and wellness become a
way of life. Make no mistake; it is not necessary or even
possible for us to *initiate* this relationship of health with
God. God first found a way to reach us. Because God did
not create us to be puppets. We can and often do resist a
relationship with him in favor of pursuing our own selfish
goals. Seeking to find God's pace for our lives focuses less
on our efforts than it does on our need for God.

When we simplify our motivations by seeking to serve
one God, we no longer have to listen to the chaotic choruses
of voices shouting for our decisions. By creating a pace that
allows our relationship with God to be "number one," we
focus more on what's important to us. The conscious choices
we make, barring any genetic or medical problems, allow
us to discover our own prescription for what ails us.

We begin to "gear down"; we no longer have to fight to
build self-esteem as we live our lives before a God who
deals with us in grace and love. As we focus on God's power,
our actions become more intentional, less susceptible to
other powers and influences. Whether we shift down, go

into high, remain in neutral, or even back up, we can remain centered on God and feeling good.

Feeling Better and Being Obedient

Just as research points out the pitfalls of a hyperpaced life-style, research also shows that focusing on God can make our bodies feel better.

Herbert Benson, author of the ground-breaking best-seller, *The Relaxation Response*, documented the effects of prayer with Catholic, Jewish, and Protestant subjects, each using a repeated phrase from their own traditions. By replacing the deluge of thoughts that sprint through a human mind with a consciously chosen sentence prayer repeated over and over in the person's mind, Benson charted an overall lower metabolic rate, slower heart rate, slower breathing, and reduced blood pressure in his subjects. Experiments indicate that this form of prayer can greatly ease headaches, hypertension, and other pain.[8]

Runners using repetitive prayer as they ran found their bodies performed more efficiently. "Aerobic prayer," with runners cadencing their pace to the rhythm of the prayer, also proved effective to many.

When Benson's study took him into the hospital to see what effects his relaxation response would have on health, he reported that "people who feel themselves in touch with God are less likely to get sick and better able to cope when they do."[9]

Few of the 102 Protestants, Jews, and Catholics who have gone through the Benson training can resist a gleeful smile over the discovery that prayer seems to do some of the things they had always hoped—and maybe a lot more—as it strengthens the spirit and heals the body.[10]

Aside from prayer, how does one begin to set aside old habits and start "gearing down?" There are shelves and racks full of the latest how-to ideas to improve our self-image, create more time, reduce stress, lose weight, win friends, and influence people. If we want to improve, there are millions of people wanting to help us. These ideas aren't necessarily bad, but we've all been down those paths. They don't always work. Not in a way that allows us to keep God central.

St. Augustine, a monk from the fifth century who struggled with his own pace until he quietly converted, said quite plainly: "You have made us for yourself and our hearts are restless until we find our rest in you."[11] St. Augustine's words help us focus in the direction this new pace will take. The question is not so much "What can I do to make myself feel better?" but rather "How can I be obedient to a God who calls me by name and claims me as his own?"

CHAPTER 5

Finding Our Pace

Therefore, since we are surrounded by so great a cloud of witnesses, let us also lay aside every weight and the sin that clings so closely, and let us run with perseverance the race that is set before us, looking to Jesus. . . .

HEBREWS 12:1, 2 (NRSV)

What drives us to an unhealthy pace of life?

What distractions keep our energies dispersed and our minds unfocused?

Drivers and Distractions

Most of us have learned "drivers" and habits of distraction from our parents and from society. We have adopted these extreme codes of conduct as basic truth. Drivers often contain the words *always* and *never*. Do any of these drivers sound familiar?

Always be strong.
Never be weak.
Never show fear.
Always work hard.
Big boys don't cry.
Never give in.
Always give in to others.
Always be nice.
Always stick to your guns.
You can have anything you set your mind to.

Trying to live up to such extreme, unrealistic guidelines can cause us great anguish. Becoming aware of these drivers reduces their influence on us. By not challenging them, we give them the power to shove more realistic thoughts out of the way. How far out of balance must the pace of our lives become before we challenge the power of a driver?

Distractions, such as concern over what people think of us, can affect us in much the same way as drivers. Their effect is proportionate to the degree of our ignorance about them. Take a moment to think about what circumstances distract you from a healthy pace of life. Some may be attitudes, such as needless worrying; others may be pastimes, such as television. Name them. If you are uncertain of the way distractions unbalance your day, carry a notebook with you for a few days and record your ups and downs.

Which of the distractions that regularly interrupt your day can you control? At the end of this chapter, you will have an opportunity to choose some strategies (pacemakers) you can use to counteract the effects of the distractions.

LIFE-STYLE SURVEY

Directions: For each of the statements in the survey below, mark one of the three possible responses. Mark AGREE if that statement is *true* or *mostly true*. Mark DISAGREE if that statement is *false* or *mostly false*. Mark UNCERTAIN sparingly, only as a last resort.

Time Management

AGREE / UNCERTAIN / DISAGREE

☐ ☐ ☐ 1. My daily private time is adequate.

☐ ☐ ☐ 2. I have a systematic way of getting most things done on time.

☐ ☐ ☐ 3. I have regular devotional times.

☐ ☐ ☐ 4. I use my private time as solitude rather than as an escape.

☐ ☐ ☐ 5. I can say no to people who ask me to do things when I'm already too busy.

☐ ☐ ☐ 6. I don't rush too much.

☐ ☐ ☐ 7. I am seldom late to my commitments.

☐ ☐ ☐ 8. I take adequate time for things I enjoy doing.

☐ ☐ ☐ 9. I seldom have too much to do.

☐ ☐ ☐ 10. I am not secretly proud of being too busy.

Family and Friends

☐ ☐ ☐ 11. I spend enough time with my loved ones.

☐ ☐ ☐ 12. When I tell people "We should get together," we usually do.

☐ ☐ ☐ 13. I have gone on a (family) vacation in the past twelve months.

☐ ☐ ☐ 14. I am rarely irritable with family and friends.
☐ ☐ ☐ 15. I have about the right amount of social activities in my life.
☐ ☐ ☐ 16. I have at least one friend with whom I can share almost anything.
☐ ☐ ☐ 17. People close to me know that I'm longing for a simpler life.
☐ ☐ ☐ 18. I consider Jesus Christ a friend of mine.
☐ ☐ ☐ 19. My family and friends support me when I want to make a change in my life.
☐ ☐ ☐ 20. I grew up in a family that valued being together.

Finances

☐ ☐ ☐ 21. I feel in control of my/our credit card debt.
☐ ☐ ☐ 22. I/we have not taken out a consolidation loan in the past twelve months.
☐ ☐ ☐ 23. My rent/mortgage payment is fairly easy to handle.
☐ ☐ ☐ 24. The way I spend my money allows me to be generous with others.
☐ ☐ ☐ 25. I/we do not spend too much money on nonessentials.
☐ ☐ ☐ 26. I have a good grasp of my/our financial status.
☐ ☐ ☐ 27. I feel comfortable with the amount of clothing I have.
☐ ☐ ☐ 28. I feel good about the percentage of my/our income I/we give to church and other good causes.
☐ ☐ ☐ 29. I/we almost never overdraw the checking account.

☐ ☐ ☐ 30. I am rarely anxious over money matters.

Physical and Emotional

☐ ☐ ☐ 31. I get adequate weekly exercise.
☐ ☐ ☐ 32. I am able to maintain a healthy weight.
☐ ☐ ☐ 33. I almost never get tension headaches or migraines.
☐ ☐ ☐ 34. I seldom feel overly anxious.
☐ ☐ ☐ 35. I do not have nervous habits.
☐ ☐ ☐ 36. I am usually calm when I drive in traffic.
☐ ☐ ☐ 37. I get adequate sleep most nights.
☐ ☐ ☐ 38. I eat healthfully.
☐ ☐ ☐ 39. I do not get minor illnesses any more often than most.
☐ ☐ ☐ 40. I seldom forget things.

General Attitudes

☐ ☐ ☐ 41. I seldom long to be somewhere else.
☐ ☐ ☐ 42. I am satisfied with most aspects of my life.
☐ ☐ ☐ 43. I could easily identify the three most important things in my life.
☐ ☐ ☐ 44. It is important for me to recycle resources where possible.
☐ ☐ ☐ 45. I know that the way I live my life has an impact on people I have never met.
☐ ☐ ☐ 46. I almost never long for a more balanced life.
☐ ☐ ☐ 47. I meet regularly with a pastor or spiritual director/guide.

☐ ☐ ☐ 48. I have previously read a book encouraging a
              simpler life-style.
☐ ☐ ☐ 49. I regularly attend worship services.
☐ ☐ ☐ 50. I consider myself an authentic and integrated
              person.

Now that you have taken the survey, please do the following:
1. Add up the total number of items you marked under
AGREE: _____

> *0–10*—You are very dissatisfied with your life-style
> and may be ready to make some immediate, sub-
> stantial changes.
>
> *11–20*—You are somewhat dissatisfied with your life-
> style and are probably longing for some significant
> changes.
>
> *21–30*—You are pleased with many areas of your life-
> style and dissatisfied with others. This may be a
> time for you to focus on a few specific aspects of
> your life.
>
> *31–40*—You are pleased with most aspects of your life-
> style and have discovered much about simplicity
> that could be shared with others.
>
> *41–50*—You have an extremely well-balanced life-
> style. How on earth do you do it? Write your own
> book and send us a copy!

2. Look more closely at your survey. In which of the five
general areas are you doing and feeling the best? Circle the
numbers of the items with which you have struggled but
have ultimately had good success.

3. Is there a general area in which you marked DISAGREE more often than others? Put a box around a few of the items on the survey in which you would especially like to see a change.

4. Are there general areas in which you marked UNCERTAIN more than two or three times? Are you aware of why this is an unresolved area for you?

5. Put an *X* on the line below to reflect whether you think your life is closer to simplicity or chaos:

SIMPLICITY _____ CHAOS

Getting a Pacemaker

You are probably lamenting about some aspects of your present life. You believe these areas to be within your control (unlike, for example, having heart disease), and you are longing for some changes. What do you do?

1. Prepare for these changes. Spend time asking God for guidance, praying, reading the Bible, and meditating in silence.

2. Make peace with the fact that the changes you make in your life-style cannot in any way earn your salvation with God. Salvation comes only by grace through faith (Rom. 3:21-26; Eph. 2:8-9).

3. Also make peace with the fact that God gave you the ability—within certain limits—to choose. (The twenty-one New Testament books from Romans to Jude are letters, many of which end with the writer

exhorting or encouraging the readers to make certain choices in how they live.)

4. In prayer, ask God to help you choose a simple personal discipline (or two or three) that will help you become more attuned to the pace God wants for you. We will call these disciplines "pacemakers." Find pacemakers that attach easily to activities already part of your routine (e.g., pray for a particular person every morning while shaving or brushing your teeth).

5. Commit yourself to your daily pacemaker(s) for at least six weeks. If, however, you find that the pacemaker(s) become other than freeing and health-giving (i.e., joyless and legalistic), set the pacemaker(s) aside until another time.

Sample Pacemakers

The following lists are not intended to be comprehensive. Rather they offer ideas for your own spiritual disciplines on your way to a simpler pace of life. Use these, adapt them, or develop your own.

Daily Pacemakers

- Begin (again?) a daily diet of Scripture reading and time of prayer. Use the devotional study in Appendix A if you like.
- Write in a journal each day. Record how your life experiences affect your faith and vice versa, how you feel about changes you are making, and similar thoughts.

- Focus on spiritual truths that nourish your faith such as these:

    I am created in the image of God.
    My Savior gave his life so that I could have abundant and eternal life.
    The Holy Spirit is prompting me to grow in wholeness.

- Exercise daily. Regular exercise such as walking is valuable for treating mild depression and generally helps people feel more alert and alive.
- Eat only three times daily and only while sitting down. This cuts out a lot of unhealthy eating habits, and unnecessary snacking.
- Drink six to eight glasses of water daily. One person we know uses those small breaks in the day to focus on his loving God.
- Breathe deeply at every stop sign or stoplight. Breathe in the blessings of God's love; breathe out that which keeps you from God's blessings.
- If you are a morning person, wake up fifteen minutes earlier than usual and spend that time in silence or in prayer. If you are a night person, set aside that special time before sleep for reflection on the day.
- Each evening think of three good things about the day and thank God for them.
- Come up with your own daily pacemakers.

Longer Range Pacemakers

- Write out your checks to church and other worthy causes before you write out checks for your bills. That way

you will tend to take your giving seriously as an important part of your budgeting process.
- Develop monthly and yearly budgets that are reasonable and not too idealistic. You may want to make use of printed resources and books on the subject to help you get started.
- Choose one evening a week or part of the weekend to enjoy being a family together—or for those living alone, to be with special friends.
- Set a limit on the amount of television you watch.
- Read a book or watch a movie that lifts your spirits—that helps you appreciate life and God's gifts.

Attaching a pacemaker, especially to the parts of our life that feel "out of pace," helps ensure space for God where God might otherwise be squeezed out. Adding pacemakers to our day helps us integrate moments of peace with moments of tension in a rhythm that flows with life. This makes "praying without ceasing" a real possibility.

Creating space for God within the busyness of our day reclaims the space God has already made for us. Whether we are fighting crowds of people at the mall, caught in traffic, or surrounded by the noises of a normal household, pacemakers allow us an opportunity to catch our breath and enjoy the presence of one who set our pace in motion.

CHAPTER 6

Keeping the Main Thing
the Main Thing

Whoever serves me must follow me.   JOHN 12:26

A dynamic speaker recently closed his remarks by saying, "The main thing is to keep the main thing the main thing."

It's amazing how a simple lack of focus can drain so much of life's energies. Some days seem like a tennis match, just trying to get that ball back across the net, meeting momentary demands with our best shot and hoping the next volley doesn't force us off the court. No matter how well we deal with each interference or distraction, sooner or later we're bound to lose a point. The result is that vague, disjointed, unfocused feeling, as though we're running in circles instead of toward the ball.

We may need to think hard to discover what really motivates us, that certain something that gets us up in the morning and keeps us moving all day. Some of us can't identify a single focus in our lives—one thing that directs our actions and motivates our decisions. We put life on autopilot. Then sometimes we feel powerless over the many circumstances that dictate our activities for the day. Something is in charge, but it's not us.

Dr. Kevin Leman says, "Getting your priorities straight and sticking to them is one of the most difficult tasks of life."[1] But if we want to regain a clearer focus, it is an essential first step.

The Oscar-winning film, *Chariots of Fire*, tells the story of Eric Liddell, an American Olympic sprinter who later became a Christian missionary to China. In the highlight race of the movie, a dramatic slow-motion sequence portrays Liddell's astounding victory while his voice rises above the action, "I believe God made me for a purpose. But he also made me fast. And when I run, I feel his pleasure."

Liddell had put his values and priorities in order. It wasn't the running that brought him the greatest pleasure; it was living in a right relationship with the Lord. That was his "main thing," and it brought him great joy.

Does the way we run life's race reflect that our relationship with God is our "main thing"? Do our values and priorities mirror loving obedience under grace? Does our faith help focus our life or does faith get lost in the blur of busyness and day-to-day routine? How well have we kept the main thing the main thing?

Many self-help books have been written to help people find their focus. A business lecturer on time management talks about the importance of finding one's "unifying factor." Richard Foster, a well-known contemporary writer and theologian, uses the word *center* to describe the "refreshing balance and equilibrium in life."

Foster says, "When we experience life at the Center, all is changed. Our many selves come under the unifying control of the divine Arbitrator. No longer are we forced to live by an inner majority rule which always leaves a disgruntled minority."[2]

Other people may use other words to describe the inner conviction that somewhere out there exists someone greater than themselves—something they can focus on, live their lives around, and maybe even worship.

Part of the problem is that God is not really "out there" at all. That restless heart, questioning who you are and why you were created, that quiet voice that keeps calling your name is not just out there, but dwells *in you*. The apostle Paul says "I pray that . . . he may strengthen you with power through his Spirit in your inner being, so that Christ may dwell in your hearts through faith" (Eph. 3:16-17).

Why Focus?

David's grandmother has used St. Charles of the Ritz products on her skin for fifty years. Needless to say, she doesn't pay much attention to the Estee Lauder advertisements or any other product that promises a youthful complexion. She knows what works for her, and she's committed to it.

We have a friend who, when finding his favorite brand of tennis shoes on sale, buys four pairs. He knows what he likes and intends to stay with it. He can make that kind of commitment because he doesn't plan on switching brands even if a new product comes on the market and demands to be bought. They can advertise all they want. He doesn't need to listen. One less voice demands his attention, and his feet are happy, too.

Many voices out there demand our attention. Sometimes we want to listen, but other times it's just excess noise or static, something to distract our mind and body. We need something to act as a filter, something that can screen out all that is not important so we can concentrate on what is.

We need a focus. A main thing. Something bigger than skin cream or tennis shoes that reminds us of the purpose of it all.

If we expect to regain a more simple heart, a more centered pace for our day, we need to order our lives in specific ways. But it is not the ordering that creates simplicity. "The things we do will not give us simplicity of heart, but they will put us in the place where we can receive it," writes Richard Foster.[3] That place of receiving is a gift—the gift of simplicity.

For the Christian, that ordering is done around the person of Jesus Christ. Out of this commitment comes a wonderful spirit of contentment. With glorious indifference to position, status, and possession, we can say no to the ridiculous pace that demands that we accumulate more. We are committed. We have a focus, and his name is Jesus.

Living Unconsciously

Life, by its very nature, doles out distractions. And frequently, just because God isn't here with audible demands as loud as the telephone or doorbell, we may displace God while we deal with the everyday details. Awareness of God may be put aside for a moment until things settle down. But do things ever settle down? Not for long. Putting God aside can become a habit with lots of good intentions tacked on.

Unless we're very careful, we can do the same things to our families. Those we love seem to be the very ones we set aside the easiest with lots of promises for the weekend. As the old song goes, "You always hurt the one you love."

God is understanding about our tendency to slight our Creator; families aren't always that forgiving.

It takes conscious effort to keep our main thing the main thing. We cannot live our lives consciously aware of God twenty-four hours a day, but we can maintain a relationship with God that exists even when we are not conscious of it. That relationship is called grace. God promises to keep us in the palm of God's hand, with or without our awareness. God has already made a space for us, even if we have not made a space for God.

Living most of our time in an unconscious state, however, is not very desirable. To say that our "main thing" exists even if we are not aware of it means that we do not have a sharp focus. We may be Christians, but our life's witness will be ineffective.

If we were to become unconscious through an accident or illness, our families could still love us, but we would not be able to love them back or relate to them in a meaningful way. If we said to our three children, "You don't have to do anything nice for us. We know you love us," it would break their hearts. They find great joy in delivering pictures of hearts and rainbows to be displayed on our refrigerator. They want the whole world to know how much they love their mom and dad.

A healthy relationship based on the grace of Jesus Christ does not preclude joyful action on our part. We heard a church leader recently speak on the subject of grace and action. He said, "Now that you don't have to do anything, what will you do?"

Our love relationship with God can lead us to take time once in awhile to draw a picture for God to hang on the refrigerator. When life's demands increase we may need to build in some specific moments, some pacemakers, that help ward off the distractions and help us remember that all-important relationship with our Creator.

The Time Is Right

The 1990s brought some dramatic changes. Some of them—especially in international politics—seemed to happen overnight. But some changes happened more slowly. Almost imperceptibly, a shift occurred in American culture from the "excessive 80s" or the "indulgent 80s," as some have called that decade, to the "inquiring 90s," termed by some the "decade of meaning." This "decade of meaning" and future meaningful decades will bring with them all sorts of societal changes involving values, beliefs, and experiences shared by the majority of society as more and more people move towards self-actualization rather than "traditionally defined success."[4]

The shift can be understood from the perspective of psychologist Abraham Maslow's list of the hierarchy of needs. More people, having met many of their physical and safety needs, are moving on toward "higher order" needs, such as self-actualization.

Role Models

Into this new framework of meaning comes an appreciation for family and an awareness that we do not live on this planet by ourselves. If the basics of life can be met for more people on a more regular basis, matters of faith begin to warrant a second look. Questions such as "Does God really exist?"; "What are the values that guide my actions?"; "What is my fair share?"; "When is enough enough?"; and "Who is my neighbor and do I really care?" begin to take the place of "How can I move up?" and "Do I have enough credit?" Society may be beginning to value people who live a more integrated life-style in which values and priorities are reflected in daily choices of food, travel, clothing, and other necessities of life. Our world needs compassionate role models who are following a call offered long ago by Christ: "Whoever serves me must follow me" (John 12:26 NRSV).

CHAPTER 7

A Call to Obedience

Go and find out what is meant by the scripture that says:
"It is kindness that I want, not . . . sacrifices."

MATTHEW 9:13 (TEV)

Anyone who travels by air has experienced the routine flight instructions that begin each leg of the journey. Flight attendants point to the nearest exits and demonstrate the use of flotation devices.

They also give special instructions concerning the oxygen masks that appear if the plane experiences a sudden drop in cabin pressure. "If you are traveling with a young child, please make sure your own oxygen mask is firmly in place before assisting the child," the flight attendant instructs. Taking care of your own needs first ensures that the child will not be left without adult aid. What would happen to the child if the adult passed out from lack of oxygen? Both lives would be in jeopardy.

If the chapters previous to this one could be compared to an airplane flight, identifying your "main thing" and implanting some specific "pacemakers" into your day means you have secured the oxygen mask over your own face. It's now time to meet the needs of the child seated next to you, a child representing two-thirds of the world's population: those who are still trying to meet Maslow's first-order needs of food, shelter, and safety.

If the values that kept us hopping around—trying to gauge our worth by how busy we were, not counting unless we were running a "they can't do it without me" pace, showcasing our business with a lot of stuff—if those values have been rearranged, prioritized, even dumped, the world will appear a different place. Our gaze will no longer focus on our own needs and what we don't have, but we will view the world as a larger place where many people's basic needs are not met.

Looking Past My Own Doorstep

It's not unusual for people with similar incomes, education, and values to become neighbors. We tend to enjoy the company of people who are like us. They make us feel more comfortable and safe. There is a problem in becoming too comfortable, however. We tend to forget those who are not like us. We tend to see the world only as we experience it. Sometimes it is good to stretch our experience even if that makes us ask uncomfortable questions.

Barbara recalls one situation that did just that.

> *The drive from the north side of town to the west didn't bother me at first. I was tutoring a Hmong woman in her home once a week while her four children ran around us, happy for some stimulation other than their parents and the three rooms of the cramped apartment. Soon the children became part of the lessons, and I started bringing M&M's as a reward for recognizing their colors.*
>
> *They had few possessions, but they were happy to be safe and free. They were even making plans for the husband to get a driver's license. They did not like to be dependent.*

As I left their apartment each week, the contrast between my home and theirs began to bother me. Four years before, we had bought the most house we could afford, looking for a good neighborhood and, probably less consciously, a place we wouldn't be ashamed of. We had found one, but it needed lots of work. No matter what I bought, I always saw something else that needed attention. No matter what I had, I thought I needed more.

As I left Mee's home each week, I had to ask myself, "How can I keep wanting more when she has so little?" Were my family's needs that much different from her family's needs? I couldn't answer those questions then. I felt uncomfortable with the whole situation and began to wonder if it wouldn't be better if I just stayed in my own neighborhood and forgot all about tutoring. I was busy enough without it.

In comparison to some, our Hmong friends "had it good." Nearly one billion members of the human family live in absolute poverty. Robert MacNamara, president of the World Bank, defines absolute poverty as "a condition of life so limited by malnutrition, illiteracy, disease, high infant mortality and low life expectancy as to be beneath any rational definition of human decency."[1]

The "one billion" statistic is incomprehensible. How do we get past the numbers and see the world with compassionate eyes?

Learning Compassion

The world cannot support a North American life-style for all who call this planet their home. Our goal cannot be to raise the standard of living so that everyone might live the way we do. There aren't enough resources. Something has to give in order for others to get. We must voluntarily, one by one, learn ways to live simply so that others may simply live. A collective action, family by family, that will challenge the "norm" can bring balance to a lopsided world and allow all the little "Annas" a chance to experience life as it was intended. It not only makes sense. It's scriptural. Some would say it's a call to obedience.

In 2 Corinthians we find one of many Scriptures that asks us to look past our own doorsteps: "Our desire is not that others might be relieved while you are hard pressed, but that there might be equality. At the present time your plenty will supply what they need, so that in turn their plenty will supply what you need. Then there will be equality, as it is written: 'He who gathered much did not have too much, and he who gathered little did not have too little' " (2 Cor. 8:13-15).

This is not a new form of socialism. It is asking those who have been blessed with many resources to be generous. It is voluntary, life-giving, and freeing—a consequence of compassionate living.

Duane Elgin, author of *Voluntary Simplicity,* further explains compassionate living. "This compassionate approach to consumption stands in stark contrast to the traditional Western view which assumes that if each of us seeks to maximize his or her personal consumption, we automatically maximize our well-being and happiness. This approach to consumption severely limits the realization of our larger human potential—individual and collective."[2]

It's not just in the 80s that we consumed an excessive amount of the world's resources. We North Americans have decades of excessive living under our belts. Even in 1953, the United States, which contained 7 percent of the world's population, produced two-thirds of its manufactured products, owned three quarters of its cars and appliances, and purchased one-third of all the goods and services available on earth.[3] The United States still uses 40 percent of all energy and minerals in the world. Is that normal living? Have we wallowed in greed so long that we have forgotten that people can live very well with much less than we have? Can we continue to consume so much more than the rest of the world and still feel comfortable?

First Steps

There is no sure-fire recipe for simple living. Various groups have tackled certain measurable areas of excessive living and gained ground. Recycling efforts have caught on everywhere. We are starting to wake up to the fact that the world has a limited ability to provide for all of us.

Although we all need to make numerous changes in our desire to own and consume, the answers to these large problems come in small decisions we make every day. Walk or ride? Meat or cheese? Glass or plastic? Paper or cloth? Shut the light off or leave it on?

The first steps matter most. The baby steps help us start walking. Somewhere, each day, someone tears the label off the soup can for the first time, removes the lid, rinses the can and saves it for the recycling center. Somewhere a few people begin to say "enough is enough," and they make that first small gesture to show they realize the world wasn't created just for them.

Compassion comes from experiencing, even in small ways, what it feels like to be without. Losing a spouse, one feels the pain more greatly for those who are alone. Watching one's family farm go on the auction block creates empathy for those who have lost possessions and homes in other circumstances.

If you have been "lucky" enough to live without air conditioning or even a fan during a hot summer season, you can know the struggle of a mother in a shantytown shack in some South American country, her baby lying listless, the heat oppressive and inescapable. If you were uncomfortable, thank God that you experienced the discomfort and pray that it might develop compassion in you for those who have no choice in the matter.

The fourth Thursday of November on most calendars in the United States is a day of feasting and giving thanks. For most it is a day of turkey with trimmings. Even in jails and soup kitchens, generous people give to help everyone eat well at least for one day.

November 15—on not as many calendars—is marked as the National Day of Fasting. A chance, at least for one day, to go without food and experience firsthand the physical forces of hunger, a body needing food and not receiving any. We are fortunate. For most of us it is just an experience and not a life-style. But it could be enough of an experience to erase the distance that separates us who "have" from the pain of those who "have not," enough to make a change and begin the process of "moving down" in some small way.

The truth of the matter is that "Anna" doesn't stand on the doorsteps of most of us. For some she lives across miles of ocean, often imprisoned by unfriendly governments. For others, she has moved across town, into bus station lobbies and homeless shelters. It is the great distance between the abundance of our lives and the emptiness of theirs that keeps us silent and distrustful, removed and unresponsive.

Yet Anna exists. It is hard to continue to live in a manner that pretends she doesn't.

God requires "kindness, not sacrifice." That is good to remember. Simplicity is not a matter of giving up things but a matter of giving. And we don't necessarily need to give up what we already have—just use what we have more wisely. Consuming our fair share of the world's resources helps the "haves" and the "have nots" draw closer together. It's peacemaking at its best. And, in the end, we all benefit.

CHAPTER 8

Half a Millennium in the Life of a Disposable Cup

*God looked at everything he had made, and he was very
pleased.* GENESIS 1:31 (TEV)

Longing for the freeing gift of a simpler, healthier life-
style for oneself leads quite naturally to a longing for that
gift for others. Our thinking can go something like this: If
what I'm discovering about simplicity is good for *me*, it is
probably also good for *us*. And if it's good for *us* it is probably
also good for *them*. (Of course, if our sense of "us" extends
to all people, then we won't have to expend energy trying
to figure out who is "us" and who is "them!")

If living simpler *personal* lives is the only goal, shouldn't
everyone simply eat from disposable plates with plastic
utensils and polystyrene cups? What could be simpler than
lifting the four corners of the tablecloth after a meal and
emptying the whole mess out the kitchen window rather
than fuss with doing dishes?

Certainly, that extreme practice would be simpler in the
short term, but it could cause health and waste problems
over the years. True simplicity needs to be a long-term
solution as well as a short-term infatuation.

Take, for example, the controversial environmental issue
of polystyrene cups. The foam cups certainly are simple

and convenient to use. But by using them, people not only cause their children to have to deal with a disposal problem—since it takes so long for polystyrene products to break down in a landfill—but, in fact, they cause problems for their children's children. Even if our lives are momentarily simplified by a disposable cup, can we justify using it if that same cup causes five hundred years of waste disposal problems? Are we not stealing a tiny opportunity for simplicity from future generations? And what of newspapers and other products that seem to last forever in a landfill?

The Bad News

Ours is a "disposable society" in which many temporary nuisances are eliminated at the earth's expense, nuisances that are simply passed on for future generations to deal with.

Here's some of the bad news (condensed from *50 Simple Things You Can Do To Save the Earth*):[1]

- It is estimated that with the arrival of the 1990s over half of America's landfills are completely full. This is not a universal problem. Other industrialized nations produce half as much trash as the United States.

- More than half of those living in the United States face possible lung damage due to polluted air.
- Some acid rain is up to 2,000 times more acidic than unpolluted rain, roughly equivalent to that of lemon juice.
- In 1983 more than a ton of hazardous waste was generated for every person in the United States.
- By the year 2000, 20 percent of all the earth's wildlife species could be extinct.
- Only 1 percent of the earth's water is usable for drinking; most of this is groundwater. Groundwater contamination has been found in all fifty states.

The United States and other countries have shown in recent decades that we are willing to go to war to protect oil interests. Are we, in fact, trying to protect humanity's "right" to extravagant use of oil and gas, which we continue to waste with barely a second thought during the conflicts? Is it possible that we as a nation are more willing to shed our young people's blood than take concrete steps to change our energy consumption habits?

We also waste a great deal of food in a world where enough food is now grown to feed all the people of the earth. Yet, incredibly, tens of thousands of people die *daily* of starvation. Some of this is due to the overconsumption of a minority of the world's population; some is due to political instability and other difficult logistics of worldwide food distribution.

Some optimistically point to a growing national awareness of environmental and global issues. In the past this seemed to be true only for as much as we are forced to deal with these issues and only for as long as we *have* to deal with them. But might it also be possible that such problems of humanity have bottomed out? That a greater awareness and a change of global heart will mean food for all in the foreseeable future?

Where Did We Go So Wrong?

One key reason we are able to abuse the earth as we do is that we forget its origin. The Genesis account of creation points to a God who surveyed all of creation and said it was *good*, or literally, it was *beautiful*.

Humankind is in danger of losing entirely this memory of the Creator's joy at the beauty of creation.

It is easy to feel crowded with the important and not-so-important demands of life: employment, cleaning the house, mowing the lawn, serving on boards and committees, doing errands, socializing, making deadlines, meeting the needs of family members, balancing the checkbook, trying to make the money go further, and countless other details. *And we can forget that God created something beautiful!*

Look Up Once in a While!

David remembers an incident some years ago.

> *I was walking back to the seminary's married student housing after a late night at the library. It was a chilly evening, and I had my head down as my heals clicked on the pavement. Suddenly, for some reason, I looked up. I remember thinking,* My goodness, there are stars. And

they're beautiful! *I had forgotten about stars—perhaps for many months. I was living my life as though there were no stars.*

Living in this world without being aware of God's creation is the spiritual equivalent of being "functionally illiterate." It is possible for people to go through all the usual training in reading and writing but still not be able to read or write. They are functionally illiterate.

An optometrist friend of ours draws a similar parallel. He identified something interesting among a handful of the Southeast Asian refugees shortly after they arrived in the United States. Some Asian people believe a person who cries too much will go blind. These people generally have had plenty of reasons to have cried, so some will function as though they are blind even though they have all the physical apparatus to have sight. For lack of a better phrase, he calls them "functionally blind."

People can also be "functionally blind" in spirit. We can have the apparatus to perceive the moving of God in our lives, but we sometimes act as though there is no God. We act as though God did not create the heavens and the earth, the creation that God called beautiful!

Our blindness is one tragic reason why we have done what we have done to God's creation.

Yet the greatest concern may not be in what has happened to creation. Damage to creation is merely a symptom of what has happened to humankind. Sadly, the polluted earth is a diary of what has happened in the human heart since the beginning of time.

Outward appearances often—but not always—express inner truths. A family counselor noted that a teenage boy he saw on a regular basis put special emphasis on cleaning and polishing his sports car. The boy openly called himself "homely" and "greasy," but he kept his car in top shape as if to say to the world, "This is what I'm *really* like on the inside."

Look at the curious mixture of good habits and bad in the way we are shaping God's creation. It is a reflection of what we are *really* like on the inside. We are created in God's image, yet we have become seriously broken and flawed by sin.

Reclaiming Two Forgotten Truths

Let's go back to the creation story in the first chapter of Genesis to clear up two common misunderstandings that have led to problems.

Many people are familiar with the first verses in the Bible: "In the beginning God created the heavens and the earth. The earth was without form and void" (Gen. 1:1-2 RSV).

For countless readers this wording has created the image that God created everything *ex nihilo* (out of nothing) immediately into its perfect and finished form. In fact, the original Hebrew indicates something more along the lines of the New Revised Standard Version: "In the beginning when God created the heavens and the earth, the earth was a formless void" (Gen. 1:1-2 NRSV). Other recent translations are similar. The idea captured here is that the raw stuff of the earth was in chaotic form when God began to sort through it and differentiate one thing from another, bringing order to chaos.

So the message of Genesis chapter one is that God created all things, and in the creating began a process of bringing order to chaos. (The word for *chaos* in Hebrew even sounds chaotic: *tohu-vavohu.*) This process took a break on the seventh day, according to the biblical record. Then comes the story of humankind's fall into sin, which introduced more chaos into the world. One might argue that much of the rest of the Bible is an account of how God continued to create, bringing order to chaos in various ways.

The importance of making this distinction in translating the first verses of Genesis is that in the more traditional versions, creation seems like a once-for-all event, but according to the original intent of the Hebrew language used, creation is a process that clearly continues on the eighth day of creation and beyond. God is still at work!

Not only does God continue creating, but from the time God asked Adam and Eve to help name the animals in the garden of Eden—and all the way through the lives of the religious leaders, prophets, teachers, rulers, and followers of Christ—God has asked people to help in bringing order to chaos. God has raised humanity above being mere creatures and invited us to be a part of the ordering and creating process.

A second common misunderstanding occurs in regard to a passage at the end of the first chapter of Genesis. According to the Revised Standard Version, God says, "Be fruitful and multiply, and fill the earth and subdue it; and have dominion" (Gen. 1:28 RSV).

One can almost hear the macho voices within us say, "Have dominion? Does that mean dominate? Why, I'll dominate this earth, all right. I'll dominate the animals, I'll dominate the forests, I'll dominate the water and the air any way I want, and, by gum, I'll dominate anyone who disagrees with me!"

The word *wasn't* dominate, though through the ages people have commonly acted as though it was. And then they used this misunderstood word as license to do whatever they wanted with creation. Professor and historian Lynn White suggests that the traditional view of having dominion makes us feel "superior to nature, contemptuous of it and willing to use it for our slightest whim."

The translation in Today's English Version (TEV) is less easily misunderstood: "I am putting you in charge of. . . ." We are, in fact, stewards of creation, even "managers of the house" as one theologian put it. We are invited into the very "house of the master" to take care of the creation. And what is a steward of God's creation supposed to do? Just what God does: bring order to the *tohu-vavohu*, to the chaos that has been around from the beginning. Once again, we are more than mere creatures; we are invited to be part of the ordering and creating process of the master of the house.

The purpose of true simplicity is not to snatch an easier life at the expense of others but to discover its freeing benefits while allowing others to experience the benefits of simplicity as well. Caring deeply for creation in thought, word, and deed helps to create in us a rich God-awareness and encourages others to follow.

Holy Dominion

David recalls an important lesson he learned from his father, a well-organized teacher, about caring for things we value.

> *My father had a desk at home that was almost always in perfect order. Pencils were sharpened, files clearly marked, everything in its place. Now and then one of my siblings or I would borrow the tape or scissors and not return them. Eventually, my father would need the missing item, track down the culprit, and give the exact same lecture. Taking us over to the desk, he would pound his hand firmly on the top and say, "Dominus sanctus!" which he loosely interpreted as* holy dominion *from the Latin. (In fact, I am told it literally means* Holy Lord.*) My father explained that he didn't intend that we never touch the desk; he just wanted us to treat it with respect. If we took something from the desk, we should remember to put it back.*

Sound advice. God's creation is also holy dominion, created by the Holy Lord. If we take something from it, let's be sure to put something back.

CHAPTER 9

We Are What
We Eat

The world can support more vegetarian Indians on bi-cycles than hamburger-eating Americans in cars.

DISCOVER, APRIL 1990

Grab your shopping cart and head down the aisle of your favorite grocery store, ready to put some of your new-found values to work in your kitchen. Eating and the choices made about what goes onto a plate and into our mouths represent more than the eater may realize. The popular phrase, *you are what you eat* takes on new meaning when applied to the problems the western diet causes for the less developed countries supplying our dietary demands.

The foods that promote personal and global health are the simple foods, according to Helen Bjornson, a public health nutritionist. These are foods that are 1) grown locally, 2) eaten as close to their natural state as possible, and 3) high in nutrition. Peas, beans, whole grains, fresh vegetables and fruit, in addition to some dairy products and small amounts of meat, ensure health for our families as well as for those who bear the brunt of production.[1]

Bjornson cautions, however, that "even simple food, like tomatoes and cantaloupe, when purchased out of season, raise concern. Faced with incredible national debt, some countries are forced to grow and export such luxury produce while their own people go hungry. Some foods, like grapes, symbolize other justice issues, and boycotts send powerful messages advocating change."[2]

In Haiti, peasants farm unproductive hillsides for their own needs while the more fertile valleys grow crops for North American supermarkets.[3] In the Philippines, families have been removed from their land and their houses bulldozed to make way for export crops to feed North Americans.[4]

Marilyn Helmuth Voran, a Mennonite and an expert on hunger issues, reports:

> *In Colombia, the largest supplier of flowers to the U.S. market, 70% of the agricultural land is controlled by a few wealthy landowners who do not experience the struggle for food most Colombians know. By growing carnations for export they reap 80% more profit per acre than by growing corn or wheat. Thus, less and less land is available for growing food for hungry Colombians.*[5]

One might guess that hunger and a desire for providing the basics for one's family has drawn into the expansive South American drug trade some poorer Colombians who might not otherwise have chosen to participate.

Voran isn't the only one making observations about how the third world responds to the western demand for low prices and maximized variety. "Shopping with a conscience can make you a basket case," an article in a publication called *SALT* declared.[6] "In the third world, farm laborers—already virtual slaves to landowners—are being exposed to chemicals so potentially deadly they have been banned in the United States. Third World rain forests and resources are also being plundered to provide Americans with 'luxury' produce, like pineapples and bananas, while Third World people starve for want of basic food crops like corn and wheat."[7]

The North American diet provides twice the recommended daily allowance for protein while other countries scramble to put added protein into their staple of rice or beans. Meat, if used at all, is used as a garnish, not as a main course around which a meal is planned.

The purpose of all this information is not to produce a sense of guilt but rather to educate all of us who feed on the sacrifices of the poor. Learning to eat more in line with the rest of the world's standards, cutting our need for excess protein and unlimited variety in or out of season, may not change the world; but one by one, as more and more people make these kinds of choices, it could produce a new demand for foods that promote both physical and moral health.

Simplicity in the supermarket is one more area affected by the call to simply live our fair share. Our overconsumption of the world's resources of food and energy supplies has left the rest of the world with a gaping wound. Realizing we can make some personal choices in an area as basic as eating, is an essential first step in the healing process.

Where To Start

Because our families will not want to be put on hold while we restructure the contents of our kitchen, there are a few simple things households can do while we acquaint ourselves with the benefits of cooking with less:

1. Eat in season. Eating some fruits and vegetables all year even when they are out of season, is like celebrating Christmas every day. Learn to appreciate the gifts of each season.
2. Choose simple foods over convenience foods. Huge amounts of time need not be spent on food preparation if the meal is built around a basic ingredient like rice or beans.
3. Purchase in bulk from local sources. By reducing excess packaging, consumers can save up to 30 percent on basic foods and cut their garbage pickup cost as well.[8]
4. Pay attention to the outside aisles of your grocery store. Most convenience foods occupy the center aisles while produce, meat, dairy, and bread items usually line the walls.
5. Start slowly. Become acquainted with a few good vegetarian menu ideas and incorporate them into your family's diet. Vegetarian chili and corn meal muffins are good starters.
6. Learn more about hunger issues. Read Arthur Simon's book, *Bread for the World,* an excellent resource for understanding the reasons for hunger and the politics that go along with it. Simon was the founder of Bread for the World, a Christian citizen's lobby on hunger issues. For more information write: Bread for the World, 802 Rhode Island Avenue, N.E., Washington, D.C. 20018.

7. Tell others. As you become more aware of the issues of hunger and the western world's response to hunger, talk about it to others. Make a commitment to educate those around you concerning the need for life-style changes and public policy changes that affect the hungry in our own countries and the world.

Arthur Simon writes:

Adopting a more modest style of life can be a powerful witness in the struggle against hunger, if efforts to change public policy accompany it . . . Not having a television set because most people in the world do not have one, or riding a bicycle to work may be morally satisfying and bring personal benefits. Unless such actions are accompanied by other positive steps, however, they accomplish nothing for hungry people . . . Life-style adjustments are sorely needed, but detached from attempts to influence government policy they tend to be ineffective gestures. Our sense of stewardship must become sufficiently large to include both.[9]

What Else Is There?

This chapter is about food choices, eating habits, and politics. The underlying purpose is to raise an awareness of how our actions affect others as well as ourselves. Similar things could have been said about clothing, transportation, or any of life's necessities. Simplicity implies an awareness of others. In many cases, it is a matter of education. "I didn't know," is different from "I didn't care." Make it a point to know. It will help you care.

"For I was hungry and you gave me something to eat, I was thirsty and you gave me something to drink, I was a stranger and you invited me in. I needed clothes and you clothed me, I was sick and you looked after me, I was in prison and you came to visit me. . . . I tell you the truth, whatever you did for one of the least of these . . . you did for me" (Matt. 25:35-36, 40).

CHAPTER 10

Come, Let Us Gather Together

For where two or three come together in my name, there am I with them.   MATTHEW 18:20

We have a framed postcard hanging in a conspicuous place in our house. It is an etching of a small sailboat heading out over choppy seas. Over the picture is written, "Dear Lord, be good to me. The sea is so wide and my boat is so small." Life's inevitable crises often cause us to wish for someone in our boat to share the struggles.

This book has been offered as an invitation to choose a simpler life-style, an opportunity to change course or at least make some alterations in the pace at which we journey. It is a journey entered into individually but best lived out corporately with others who share our values and reasons for change.

Tilden Edwards, author of *Living Simply Through the Day: Spiritual Survival in a Complex Age*, writes about the importance of sharing our journey with others:

> *Unless we are particularly heroic or saintly persons, each of us needs a relationship with at least one other person who also seeks and trusts the simple way, the Simple Presence. Such a "spiritual friend" can be enormously supportive to*

us, and we to them. Even if you meet or write to each other only once a month, it can be enough. Just knowing that someone else is struggling for the simple day with you, whether or not you speak together often, is encouraging. You feel a little less alone, a little less tempted to fall mindlessly into complicating traps. Someone else is there who knows whether or not you are trying to pay attention to the simple way; that brings a kind of accountability that is important. When someone else knows and cares, then we pay that much more attention to what we're doing.[1]

On the Judging Block

To be honest, we haven't always felt terribly encouraged in our decision to live more simply. In the beginning we got some pats on the back from some who saw it as a good thing, but those pats of encouragement were given with long arms—from a distance. Other people were a bit more assertive, wondering how we could take our kids to Disneyworld when we were trying to live a more simple calling.

That is a danger in choosing to cut loose some of the trappings of a society that tends to overindulge. Sometimes you end up on the judging block. The conversation goes something like this: "If you don't want it all, then you must not want any of it." We wish it were that easy. What we wanted to find was a life-style that didn't control us either financially or emotionally. A life-style that allowed us to be generous and less wasteful. A life-style that allowed us to laugh more and love more greatly. We cut back. We didn't move into a mud hut. Our children still eat fast food occasionally.

But sometimes our decisions leave us feeling a bit lonely. After our move, we didn't feel as comfortable with our former neighbors. Perhaps some people thought we were going to lay a heavy "You should be doing this" on them. We didn't. More than likely, any uncomfortable feelings we felt about "not fitting in" were our own. We had a lot of questions but few people with whom to discuss them. We needed a community. What we got was Michaela.

A Good Friend

A sharp turn right at the crest of Priory Road took us down a newly paved drive to what once housed a private girls' school. St. Bede Priory and Ecumenical Center now provides home to sixty-seven Benedictine sisters, one of whom is called Sister Michaela.

Michaela, prioress of St. Bede, found us in the library on the third floor of the center. She was there to explain the Benedictine community as best she could, considering we were not Catholic. Immediately, she showed concern for our comfort. "Would you like to stay here and work?" she asked. "We could talk in the other room if you like."

Hospitality is a key word at St. Bede or in any Benedictine community. They have been practicing hospitality in Christ's name for over 1500 years, and they are very good at it.

We settled down to define monastic life in Protestant jargon.

"The monastic way of life is a way of living a 'rule' and is lived out in community," she said. We listened and observed. It was hard to tell Michaela's age. Her hair appeared prematurely gray. But her timeless eyes laughed as she reflected back a few years.

"I went to Australia several years ago, and people there were saying, 'You can't be Benedictine. Benedictines are monastic.' "

She explained the confusion. Monastic at one time meant cloistered. Today, it also means contemplative. "You don't have to be cloistered to be contemplative." She smiled. "We are all contemplative. There is an archetype of a monk in all of us."

It seemed strange that a couple with three children—a family like ours—could find any similarities with the life-style of a contemplative sister. We did. Michaela had an understanding of an integrated life that modeled some of the elements we wanted in our own lives.

There is an integration of work and prayer in the Benedictine community that models their way of living. Defining work as both manual and intellectual, the Benedictines are the first monastic order, it is said, to get dirt under their fingernails. Along with their work, they pray. Their schedule is one very aware of human nature.

"If one is to draw back from speaking or eating or even laughing," Michaela told us, "it would only seem appropriate that there are times to bring those things back into one's life. In order to draw back from something, it must be present in the first place."

The phone rang while Michaela was speaking. She talked all the way to the phone and let it ring an extra time as she finished her thought. It felt good not to be put on hold.

When she got back, we discussed the life of St. Benedict and the impact of Vatican II, and we talked about and

defined obedience as "listening with the ear of your heart."
We paused and we listened. It felt good to have a friend.

Community in Many Forms

Michaela offered and continues to offer us her insights
and prayers. For us, she is a spiritual community of one,
and we are thankful to have her.

The benefits of community can also be found with family,
friends, and our own congregations. The disciplines asso-
ciated with community can take the form of the very complex to the very simple.

Members of the Order of Saints Martin and Teresa
(OSMT), an ecumenical collection of people committed to
peacemaking, call themselves a "family of individuals and
communities committed to following Christ by (1) observing
spiritual disciplines and (2) working for reconciliation
through nonviolent peacemaking. OSMT is committed to
active and reconciling nonviolence, theological reflection,
and meditation. These values are kept alive by three daily
disciplines or practices: wearing a paper clip, keeping a
journal and taking a walk."[2]

OSMT members are loosely linked by a mailing list.
Members receive a quarterly devotional booklet. It is not
a highly structured membership list, but there is an annual
gathering for those who can attend. They'll send us their
journals even if we don't promise to wear the paper clip.

What makes them worth studying is their sense of community. The paper clip, journal, and daily walk are simple
commitments to a daily practice, ensuring a conscious
awareness of God. They are good examples of what we have

called pacemakers. Their chosen disciplines are enhanced by the fact that others, on a daily basis, are sharing these three activities with them—people whose names they do not even know.

Putting on a paper clip each morning reminds them to make a renewed commitment to nonviolence. OSMT chose this symbolic practice, following the example of Norwegian children who wore a paper clip each day as a sign of their resistance to the Nazi regime. Daily journaling is an exercise in connecting faith and life. A brief walk is one way to have time each day for solitude and meditation. These are not laws. No one is going to "kick you out" if you don't take your walk. Their practices or disciplines are done from a sense of values and because they simply find them helpful.

Living out our faith, connected with others who share similar values, could define the activity of nearly any healthy congregation. Almost any church already expresses itself through a few shared disciplines: hearing God's Word, baptism, holy communion, prayer, worship. If we are Christians and members of a congregation, we have already experienced in some ways the support of a community of believers.

Levels of Community

Ernest Boyer, in his book, *Finding God at Home*, defines three levels of community, each building on the first.[3]

Boyer labels the first level of community, *forming ties*. This describes the times when small groups of people gather together on a regular basis to learn more about each other. It may be over dinner or for no other reason than to enjoy one another. Whether its members are consciously aware of themselves as a community is not important. They have broken out of the isolation and begun to form ties.

The second level, *joining lives,* is reached when the members of a community recognize the sense of community that already exists, such as when those in an ongoing Bible study become good friends and support each other in times of illness or grief. An interdependence has developed. The ties are not so much changed as appreciated in a new and deeper way. Good social acquaintances move toward deeper friendships. Bonds grow stronger.

Union marks the third level of community. Boyer writes:

> *[Union] is when the differences between people are no longer barriers, not because they have been somehow washed away, but because they have become so fully accepted that no one would even think to hide them. Union can occur at all levels of community . . . It is something that comes and goes. It does this not because we as humans are so imperfect, but because we as humans have such a hard time accepting those imperfections in ourselves and in others.*[4]

Trying It On

Jesus did not live a life of isolation. He found twelve good friends, all with different personalities and gifts, to support him in his ministry. They weren't always successful. Sometimes they doubted him. Sometimes they denied they knew him. Friends, even chosen friends, can be cruel. Despite their brokenness, Jesus taught them, encouraged them, and prayed for them. When he died, at least one stood at the foot of his cross and did not hide. A community of believers.

Opening ourselves to people, especially for support, is a risky thing. But community, no matter how we choose to encourage it in our own lives, is worth the risk. Without it, we become isolated, bitter, and resentful.

In the beginning, God created Adam. God saw that it was not good for the man to live in the garden alone, so God created Eve. God's been making community ever since. It continues to be very good.

"Dear God, help us tear down the walls between people. Help us to replace distrust with openness, separation with sharing, fear with love. It is you who becomes the bond that connects people. Teach us to know you enough to seek that connection. Save us, God, from isolation."[5]

CHAPTER 11

When I Feel
Like a Failure

I do not understand my own actions. For I do not do what I want, but I do the very thing I hate. Wretched man that I am! Who will rescue me from this body of death? ROMANS 7:15, 24 NRSV

It's easy to become interested in a simpler life-style. Even people who have yet to make any definite commitment to life-style changes tell us they are intrigued with the concept as we were when we first began reading about this very personal and important topic.

Like us, perhaps you want to put your insights and good intentions into action. So you start to make life-style changes that you know will be good and freeing for you in so many ways. You know it will make those you love pleased to see you becoming a more balanced and integrated person. And, of course, you expect all these changes to please God, too.

But then (dramatic music, please: dum de dum dum) . . . you *fail!*

You intended to follow through with your goal of having some quiet time each day to focus on the Scriptures in the back of this book, you intended to keep recycling, to change your hurried attitude, to eat more wisely, to take time for the things you say are important to you, to spend more time with your loved ones.

Shame and disappointment descend like a fog. You envision your own gravestone with the all-too-true phrase added just under your name, "This person meant well, but alas. . . ." You get angry at yourself, like the person on a diet who "blows it" by ordering out for a midnight pizza. Since you have told close friends about your intent to make changes in your life, you try to hide your failure from them, much as an alcoholic hides bottles in the dark places of the house.

Then you get hit with the dreaded all-or-none thinking: "If I can't do it right the first time, then forget it. Just forget it all!"

There are some nagging, powerful lessons in the above scenarios.

We Will Fail

Take comfort in an unusual thought: we *will* fail.

The New Testament book of Romans has a wonderful way of dealing with the struggle between flesh and spirit, addressing the fact that what we do doesn't always match what we want to do.

The apostle Paul, a hero of the New Testament who wrote more books of the Bible than any other writer, wrote brilliantly about this noble struggle within himself. "I do not understand my own actions. For I do not do what I want, but I do the very thing I hate. . . . For I delight in the law of God in my inmost self, but I see in my members another law at war with the law of my mind, making me captive to the law of sin that dwells in my members" (Rom. 7:15, 22-23 NRSV).

So we've struggled. We've failed. But it seems we're in good company.

In case we have any continuing elitist feelings that perhaps our ability to be godly in all things is a notch higher than others, let's take a look at a bit more of Paul's letter to the Romans. "None is righteous, no, not one; no one understands, no one seeks for God. All have turned aside, together they have gone wrong; no one does good, not even one" (Rom. 3:10-12, RSV).

With that kind of a human pedigree, we will most assuredly fail at some point with even our best intentions for a healthier life-style.

But failing and being a failure are two different things. At the height of Paul's doubt about his ability to follow through on his best intentions, he says, "Wretched man that I am! Who will deliver me from this body of death?" (Rom. 7:24 RSV). The answer comes in Romans 8:1: "There is therefore now no condemnation for those who are in Christ Jesus."

We may fail in our intentions, but those who are "in Christ Jesus" are anything but failures in God's eyes.

Even in the world's eyes—that is, in a secular sense—failing does not mean failure. The average "self-made" millionaire does not waltz into success. Many of them had to declare bankruptcy (experience extreme financial failure) at least once before coming into their millions.

We will fail in our good intentions to live a more simple life-style. And we will fail again. And we will fail again. And again. And . . . We get the point. But remember two things: (1) we are never an utter failure in God's eyes, and (2) freed of the necessity to succeed, we will find that we

have the ability to persist again and again. And again. And
. . . We get the idea. It won't happen all at once. But it
will happen.

Strategies to Help Us Persist

Strategy #1—Realize that new practices take about
six weeks to become habits. Allow at least that much
time before deciding if the desired changes are possible or not.

Strategy #2—Realize that God is more patient with
us than we are with ourselves. Many of us have
negative images of God: an angry, white-bearded
old man on a distant throne; a critical, disapproving
parent figure; an unforgiving taskmaster in the faith.
Just at the time we need a shepherd to guide us,
our guilt creates God in the image of a Marine drill
sergeant.

Strategy #3—Identify the source of all the negative,
"failure" feelings. Many of us have "tapes" in our
heads, recorded in our childhood, that still affect
how we see ourselves. If we can identify the negative messages, they won't have as severe an effect
on how we perceive ourselves today.

Strategy #4—Set appropriate goals. If we feel like a
failure, perhaps we have tried to accomplish too
much all at once. Select smaller, more measurable
goals and objectives. For example, trying to get rid
of all your excess belongings in one week might be
difficult. Try pruning back just one closet or room
at a time.

Strategy #5—Regularly examine attitudes. We need to periodically ask ourselves if we have been too grim and joyless in our attempts at meaningful lifestyle changes. If we have succeeded only in setting up a new set of weighty laws that are hard to live up to, we need to set them all aside for a while. Channel the desire for change into many opportunities for celebration and fun.

Leaders of The Haiti Project, a Wisconsin-based group trying to eliminate hunger in Haiti by the year 2000, schedule picnics, entertainment, and family hikes as part of their agenda to deal with their serious task. "If we don't do this with some fun and a sense of humor," the chairperson says, "odd as that may seem, people may not stick with the goal."

Strategy #6—Develop a proper perspective about what we are attempting. In one sense, the way we choose to live and the things we choose to do are very important. On the other hand, Jesus Christ has already done what is *really* important, don't you think?

Strategy #7—Don't let the knowledge that we will fail be an excuse not to start.

Failing Isn't All Bad

North Americans don't like failing. In business and sports and a hundred other places, our society rewards winners—those who succeed. And so we do our best to maintain the illusion of success, even if it is costly.

There are, however, some clear benefits to admitting the truth about where we are weak. People who know where they are weak know what they need to work on and may one day overcome that problem. Are you having trouble feeling compassion for the underprivileged in other countries? Admit your problem. Then treat yourself to a trip— not the touristy kind that hits twelve major European cities in ten days, but instead go to a developing nation and visit some missionaries from your denomination.

Our friend Bob Swenson found the increasing failure of his body to be a time of spiritual renewal. Bob had Lou Gehrig's Disease, and as his body's nervous system degenerated, he gradually lost control of his muscles. Ultimately, though he was unable to move anything but his eyelids, he was experiencing monumental growth in spirit and character. Just months before he died, he signaled with his eyes to a letter board: "I have dedicated my life to witness of my Lord Jesus." His life became *really* simple, but he saw that as a time to grow. Failing time was opportunity time for Bob Swenson.

Failing time can be good for us, too. God's Word to Paul is God's Word to us. "My grace is sufficient for you, for my power is made perfect in weakness" (2 Cor. 12:9, RSV).

One special hazard faced by people seeking a simpler life is that the desire to "keep up with the Joneses" doesn't automatically go away. But just as the greatest courage is not a lack of fear but the ability to persist in spite of it, so the greatest simplicity is not a lack of envy but the ability to persist in spite of it.

A 1989 article in *Psychology Today* reminds us that

although painful, once owned up to, envy can be transformed from a detour into a spur to action . . . It may mean it's time to accept material limits, or growing older and losing physical advantages once taken for granted. It may lead to a change of values, a shift to a less materialistic, more spiritual or fulfilling view of life. Such explorations can resolve the painful dilemma of envy—and offer new challenges and opportunities for growth.[1]

Persist, Persist, Persist

The secret to reaching most worthwhile goals is simply to persist and persist and persist.

We who seek simpler life-styles that will give us greater integrity and health need the grace and courage to begin. Can we allow a redirection of our lives for six weeks? Will we allow this growth to continue for a lifetime? Will we readily share with others who show an interest in finding a new pace for their lives?

Share your life-style adventure with others when they ask. And be hopeful. In this desire for new beginnings we are not alone.

"Have reverence for Christ in your hearts, and honor him as Lord. Be ready at all times to answer anyone who asks you to explain the hope you have in you, but do it with gentleness and respect" (1 Pet. 3:15-16 TEV).

CHAPTER 12

Enlisting in the Magnificent Conspiracy

Being confident of this, that he who began a good work in you will carry it on to completion until the day of Christ Jesus. PHILIPPIANS 1:6

*C*onspiracy—to combine or work together for a purpose.

This book has not been as much a how-to book as a why-to book. The "how to" comes as readers begin to form their own conspiracy against an overindulgent society by reclaiming their own values and living by them. It is a conspiracy entered into individually but best lived out corporately with others who share similar values and reasons for change. And this conspiracy finds its roots in the very teachings of Jesus and the Scriptures on which we base our faith.

Jesus tells a rather grim parable in Luke 12:15-21:

> *Then he [Jesus] said to them, "Watch out! Be on your guard against all kinds of greed; a man's life does not consist in the abundance of his possessions."*
>
> *And he told them this parable: "The ground of a certain rich man produced a good crop. He thought to himself, 'What shall I do? I have no place to store my crops.'*
>
> *"Then he said, 'This is what I'll do. I will tear down my barns and build bigger ones, and there I will store all*

*my grain and my goods. And I'll say to myself, "You have
plenty of good things laid up for many years. Take life easy;
eat, drink and be merry.' "*

*But God said to him, "You fool! This very night your
life will be demanded from you. Then who will get what you
have prepared for yourself?"*

*This is how it will be with anyone who stores up things
for himself but is not rich toward God.*

We would not feel comfortable personalizing this piece
of Scripture. Who wants to be called a fool for the choices
they have made? Jesus does not mean to be cruel in this
passage. He does not use scare tactics. But Jesus is very
practical. He calls it as he sees it. And sometimes it isn't
easy to hear what he is trying to tell us.

Our daughter, in her younger years, had "discriminatory
hearing." She often had trouble hearing directions about
shutting off television or coming for supper, but a whispered
promise of a trip to the Dairy Queen needed no reminder.
On one particular day, after issuing multiple requests for
her to pick up her toys, we suddenly realized she was missing. After a frantic search of the house, we found her hiding
under her bed, her hands over her ears. "Oh!" she said
sweetly in response to our startled silence, "I didn't hear
you."

It's a little embarrassing—even to a four-year-old—to be
found hiding under a bed trying not to hear what is being
asked of us. Can we honestly look Jesus in the eye and say,
"Oh, I didn't hear you"? The truth of the matter is, we
don't always want to hear. Hearing threatens too much
change. It stirs uncomfortable feelings. No one likes to feel

uncomfortable, especially when it comes to faith and its place in our everyday lives.

What is God's response to us if we do not listen to his teachings? Probably the same as ours when we found our little girl hiding in her bedroom. We smiled, understanding childish ways. We still loved her. Whether she listened or not, she remained a loved and cherished child. God loves us even more than that.

But we are adults. We pick up our toys now, even when no one asks. We try not to cover our ears when asked the hard questions. We choose either to be obedient to God's truth as we understand it or to remain hiding under the covers, trying hard not to hear.

Learning to Listen

For both of us, our decision to join this magnificent conspiracy called simplicity came as a direct result of Bible study and subsequent discussions with friends. The Scriptures continue to amaze us with their ability to transform lives and move hearts. Scripture is for us the clearest manner in which God addresses us. Every time we enter some form of Bible study we come away changed and redirected. It's an amazing thing!

Because we believe this so firmly, we want to suggest a six-week study, an immersion into some of the Scriptures that guided us toward some new beginnings. The Bible is a good place to start as you consider joining this magnificent conspiracy called simplicity.

The daily Scripture and prayer that are given in the upcoming pages may be followed by your own reflection either by writing in a journal (a notebook, diary, or blank book) or by remaining in silence for a few minutes after your devotional time. Listen. Don't be afraid to feel uncomfortable. Those restless feelings signal the beginning of change. Feeling uncomfortable is not a bad thing if it moves us toward wholeness.

You may find it helpful during your time of reflection to ask yourself the following questions:

- "How does this Scripture make me feel?"
- "What is the Lord trying to say in this passage?"
- "Where am I to go from here?"

It helps if you can attach this assignment, short as it is, to something you already do—eating a meal or reading at bedtime. As you read the Scriptures, slow your pace. What word(s) pop out at you? Where did you naturally want to stop and reflect?

We have included six weeks of Scriptures here because it takes about six weeks to establish any new habit. In other words, after you followed a new habit for six weeks or more, something will not seem quite right if you skip a day. The new habit has become the norm. We hope that daily Scripture reading can become a habit for you as you begin to listen and learn.

Thankful for the Gift

Simplicity is more than slowing down. It is a life-style chosen not only for personal benefits but for the important statement it makes to the world family. In slowing our own pace of consumption we eliminate from our lives some of the excesses that keep us running to meet their needs. Simplicity is a way to take charge of our own lives and quit trying to meet the false expectations society imposes.

For many of us who have been living life on cruise control, a switch to manual requires some startling changes as we create a new vision for our life's potential. A clearer understanding emerges: our day-to-day choices *do* matter; there are consequences to *every* action or lack of action.

Simplicity requires a conspiracy of sorts—a magnificent conspiracy with world-wide implications. When people begin to embrace the gospel—not just believe it but live it out—people get fed, children find homes, and families find peace. These are just some of the gifts of simplicity.

In some ways this book is a never-ending story. The next chapters may never be written on paper but they will be lived out in the lives of individuals who make daily choices towards a more simple life. We encourage you to live with eyes for the world instead of worldly eyes. And we remind you to turn your eyes upon Jesus, too. Blessings on your journey.

"Behold, I make all things new." REV. 21:5 KJV

Six-Week Scripture Reflection on Simplicity

WEEK ONE

DAY 1: The world and all that is in it belong to the LORD; the earth and all who live on it are his.   Ps. 24:1 TEV
PRAYER: You came for all, Lord. Not just for me or my family. Not just for those who live near me. Not just for people in my denomination. Not just for North Americans. You came for all your children, and like a good parent you have no favorites. AMEN.

DAY 2: LORD, how happy is the person you instruct, the one to whom you teach your law!   Ps. 94:12 TEV
PRAYER: Make me a willing learner. Open my heart and mind to hear your voice. Teach me your ways, oh Lord. AMEN.

DAY 3: As he saw the crowds, his heart was filled with pity for them, because they were worried and helpless, like sheep without a shepherd.   MATT. 9:36 TEV

PRAYER: Teach me to see the crowds, Lord, and not just walk through them. In the shopping malls and in five-o'clock traffic, teach me compassion. AMEN.

DAY 4: When he cries out to me for help, I will answer him because I am merciful. EX. 22:27B TEV
PRAYER: I suppose you cried that night in the manger, Jesus. Just because people get big doesn't mean they stop crying. It just sounds different. Sometimes it comes out in angry words. Sometimes it comes out in violence. Help us to hear the cries, Lord, and to be compassionate. AMEN.

DAY 5: God said, "See, I have given you every plant yielding seed that is upon the face of all the earth, and every tree with seed in its fruit; you shall have them for food." GEN. 1:29 NRSV
PRAYER: Thank you, Lord, that you provide for us such great variety of food and the seed for it to continue. I am overwhelmed at your goodness. AMEN.

DAY 6: So my counsel is: Don't worry about *things*—food, drink, and clothes. . . . Look at the birds! They don't worry about what to eat . . . for your heavenly Father feeds them. And you are far more valuable to him than they are. MATT. 6:25-26 TLB
PRAYER: When I feel like worrying or complaining, help me lift my thoughts to you, Jesus. Thank you for all you have provided. AMEN.

DAY 7: And God is able to give you more than you need, so that you will always have all you need for yourselves and more than enough for every good cause. 2 COR. 9:8 TEV

PRAYER: If I have more than I need, why is it so hard to help someone else who doesn't? Is it because I'm afraid that you really won't supply all my needs? You promised, Lord. I believe you. Help me to share freely without fear. AMEN.

WEEK TWO

DAY 1: There was a man all alone; he had neither son nor brother. There was no end to his toil, yet his eyes were not content with his wealth. "For whom am I toiling," he asked, "and why am I depriving myself of enjoyment?" This too is meaningless—a miserable business! ECCL. 4:8
PRAYER: Help me get my priorities straight, Lord. For whom do I work? Give me the joy of working for you. AMEN.

DAY 2: Listen to what is wise and try to understand it. Yes, beg for knowledge; plead for insight. Look for it as hard as you would for silver or some hidden treasure. . . . If you listen to me, you will know what is right, just, and fair. PROV. 2:2-4, 9 TEV
PRAYER: Lord, you give wisdom, and from your mouth comes knowledge and understanding. Teach me to listen. AMEN.

DAY 3: Trust in the LORD with all your heart. Never rely on what you think you know. Remember the LORD in everything you do, and he will show you the right way. PROV. 3:5-6 TEV

PRAYER: What does it really mean to trust you, Lord? Keep your presence ever near and teach me to live my life as you lived yours. AMEN.

DAY 4: No pupil is greater than his teacher; no slave is greater than his master. So a pupil should be satisfied to become like his teacher, and a slave like his master. MATT. 10:24-25 TEV
PRAYER: Make me your pupil, Jesus. Help me look to you for instruction and guidance. AMEN.

DAY 5: "Then let us no more pass judgment on one another, but rather decide never to put a stumbling block or hindrance in the way of a brother.   ROMANS 14:13 RSV
PRAYER: Help me evaluate my life, Lord, that it may glorify you. AMEN.

DAY 6: Give me neither poverty nor riches; feed me with the food that is needful for me.   PROV. 30:8 RSV
PRAYER: Where is the line, Lord? When is enough enough? What is my fair share? Teach me, Lord. AMEN.

DAY 7: Create in me a clean heart, O God, and put a new and right spirit within me.   PS. 51:10 NRSV
PRAYER: Do not cast me away from your presence, and do not take your holy spirit from me. Restore to me the joy of your salvation, and sustain in me a willing spirit (PS. 51:11-12). AMEN.

WEEK THREE

DAY 1: Happy are the pure in heart; they will see God! MATT. 5:8 TEV

PRAYER: It is true, God. Every time I clear away the
clutter, the activity, the busyness—every time I pause to
see the good, I see you, God, and I give thanks. AMEN.

DAY 2: Therefore, since we are surrounded by such a great
cloud of witnesses, let us throw off everything that hinders
and the sin that so easily entangles, and let us run with
perseverance the race marked out for us.   HEB. 12:1
PRAYER: Cut away the things that entangle me, Lord,
and help me to run life's race unencumbered. AMEN.

DAY 3: Go and learn what this means, "I desire mercy, not
sacrifice."   MATT. 9:13 TEV
PRAYER: Teach me the difference between doing something for the effect and doing something out of obedience.
Motivate me to act in kindness. Keep my actions less self-
aware. AMEN.

DAY 4: Jesus sat down, called the twelve disciples, and said
to them, "Whoever wants to be first must place himself last
of all and be the servant of all."   MARK 9:35 TEV
PRAYER: You knew what it meant to be last, Lord. Born
in a barn to poor parents, no prestige, few possessions. We
expected to follow a king. Help us learn to follow a servant.
AMEN.

DAY 5: "If anyone wants to come with me," he told them,
"he must forget himself, carry his cross, and follow me."
MARK 8:34 TEV
PRAYER: Help me to remember that your love is free but
following you can be very expensive. AMEN.

DAY 6: You know the grace of our Lord Jesus Christ; rich as he was, he made himself poor for your sake.
2 COR. 8:9 TEV
PRAYER: I thank you, Jesus, for coming to us a human being. I thank you for becoming one of us. When I think of that, I am humbled by your love. AMEN.

DAY 7: Don't let the world around you squeeze you into its own mold.   ROMANS 12:2 PHILLIPS
PRAYER: Who sets the standards, Lord? TV keeps telling us to buy, buy, buy. Commercials fill the kids' heads with brand names. Help us keep life simple, Lord. Help us break the mold. AMEN.

WEEK FOUR

DAY 1: Jesus called his disciples to him and said, "I feel sorry for these people, because they have been with me for three days and now have nothing to eat."
MATT. 15:32 TEV
PRAYER: Fill me with compassion, Lord, as you fill my stomach with food. Remind me that there are those with hungry hearts as well as hungry stomachs. Help me share my food and my companionship. AMEN.

DAY 2: Zacchaeus stood up and said to the Lord, "Listen, sir! I will give half my belongings to the poor, and if I have cheated anyone, I will pay him back four times as much!"   LUKE 19:8 TEV
PRAYER: How much of what I have is really mine, Jesus? Is it right for some to have so much while others have so

little? Help me not to define a "good deal" as when someone else pays. Help me to be fair. AMEN.

DAY 3: I can assure you that they gave as much as they could, and even more than they could . . . they begged us and pleaded for the privilege of having a part in helping God's people"   2 COR. 8:3-4 TEV
PRAYER: Thank you for the many opportunities you give us to honor you by helping others. Teach us to be kind to all God's people. AMEN.

DAY 4: I am not trying to relieve others by putting a burden on you; but since you have plenty at this time, it is only fair that you should help those who are in need.
2 COR. 8:13-14 TEV
PRAYER: Sometimes I don't realize I have plenty, Jesus. Sometimes it seems like everyone else has more. Relieve me from the burden of wanting, and teach me to share. AMEN.

DAY 5: The Spirit of the Lord is upon me, because he has chosen me to bring good news to the poor. He has sent me to proclaim liberty to the captives . . . to set free the oppressed and announce that the time has come when the Lord will save his people.   LUKE 4:18-19 TEV
PRAYER: When we ask you what we can do, Lord, hand us this job description from Luke 4 and tell us you're recruiting. AMEN.

DAY 6: The people asked him, "What are we to do, then?" He answered, "Whoever has two shirts must give one to the man who has none, and whoever has food must share it." LUKE 3:10-11 TEV

PRAYER: You spoke simply, Lord. Help me not to theologize, devotionalize, or generalize so much that I miss the point. Help me to simply hear you and obey. AMEN.

DAY 7: All the believers continued together in close fellowship and shared their belongings with one another. They would sell their property and possessions, and distribute the money among all, according to what each one needed. ACTS 2:44-45 TEV

PRAYER: People keep asking me what I want for my birthday or Christmas. Lord, there are a lot of things I want but not many things I really need. Help me learn the difference between what I want and what I need. AMEN.

WEEK FIVE

DAY 1: But his answer was: "My grace is all you need." 2 COR. 12:9 TEV

PRAYER: Sometimes I get discouraged when I really just need to be content. Teach me contentment, Lord, but help me not to be complacent. Break through the confusion and simplify my heart. AMEN.

DAY 2: Now this is our boast: Our conscience testifies that we have conducted ourselves in the world, and especially in our relations with you, in the holiness and sincerity that are from God. We have done so not according to worldly wisdom but according to God's grace. 2 COR. 1:12

PRAYER: God, create in me a need to treat others with holiness and sincerity. Help me see that all life has value and worth. AMEN.

DAY 3: He will always make you rich enough to be generous at all times, so that many will thank God for your gifts which they receive from us. For this service you perform not only meets the needs of God's people, but also produces an outpouring of gratitude to God.   2 COR. 9:11-12 TEV

PRAYER: Whose standards declare me rich? When I compare myself to those who have more than I do, I just want more. When I compare myself to those who have little, I am content and humbled. Humble my heart, Lord. AMEN.

DAY 4: Remember how it was with you in the past, in those days after God's light had shone on you, you suffered many things yet were not defeated by the struggle. You were at times publicly insulted and mistreated, and at other times you were ready to join those who were being treated in this way . . . you endured your loss gladly, because you knew that you still possessed something much better, which would last forever.   HEB. 10:32-34 TEV

PRAYER: I am not always so ready to join those who are being mistreated. That's a hard one. Ask me to feel compassion. Ask me for money. But to join them would mean a change in life-style. If this is what you desire for me, help me be willing. Thank you, Lord, that *you* were willing to change your life-style and join us. AMEN.

DAY 5: Lift up your tired hands, then, and strengthen your trembling knees! Keep walking on straight paths, so that

the lame foot may not be disabled, but instead be healed.
HEB. 12:12-13 TEV
PRAYER: Remove the barriers that separate us by possessions and wealth. Make level my path so that how I live does not disable another. AMEN.

DAY 6: So then, have your minds ready for action. Keep alert and set your hope completely on the blessing which will be given you when Jesus Christ is revealed. Be obedient to God, and do not allow your lives to be shaped by those desires you had when you were still ignorant.
1 PET. 1:13-14 TEV
PRAYER: The trouble with simplicity, Lord, is that it requires an R.S.V.P. It would be easier never to have received the invitation. Speak to my heart, Lord. Encourage me. AMEN.

DAY 7: I am sure, as I write this, that you will do what I ask—in fact I know that you will do even more.   PHIL. 1:21 TEV
PRAYER: I have heard your message and seen your example, Lord. Help me to be obedient. Fill me with kindness. Teach me to live your gospel. AMEN.

WEEK SIX

DAY 1: I was hungry and you fed me, thirsty and you gave me a drink; I was a stranger and you received me in your homes, naked and you clothed me; I was sick and you took care of me, in prison and you visited me.
MATT. 25:35-36 TEV

PRAYER: I can't meet everyone's needs, Lord. Show me how to direct my resources to do the greatest good. Help me offer what you have first given me—myself, my time, and my possessions. AMEN.

DAY 2: The King will reply, "I tell you, whenever you did this for one of the least important of these brothers of mine, you did it for me!" MATT. 25:40 TEV
PRAYER: Lord, let me see your face in every face. Let my every act be an act of worship in praise of you, heavenly Father. AMEN.

DAY 3: Whoever welcomes you welcomes me; and whoever welcomes me welcomes the one who sent me.
MATT. 10:40 TEV
PRAYER: I welcome so many during the year: relatives, friends, and you, Lord. Let every person feel a sense of welcome from someone today. Help me welcome others as I welcome you once again into my heart. AMEN.

DAY 4: Whoever tries to gain his own life will lose it; but whoever loses his life for my sake will gain it.
MATT. 10:39 TEV
PRAYER: Any change brings some grief. Help me to expect to grieve, Lord. Be with me in my sadness. Comfort me with your presence. AMEN.

DAY 5: He has told you, O mortal, what is good; and what does the Lord require of you but to do justice, and to love kindness, and to walk humbly with your God?
MIC. 6:8 NRSV

PRAYER: I pray for those who have little power—children, the elderly, the poor. Help those *with* power to be kind and compassionate. Help me to use my own power wisely. AMEN.

DAY 6: Come to me, all you that are weary and are carrying heavy burdens, and I will give you rest. Take my yoke upon you, and learn from me; for I am gentle and humble in heart, and you will find rest for your souls. For my yoke is easy, and my burden is light. MATT. 11:28-30 NRSV

PRAYER: Lord, you continue to invite me. You continue to tell me who you are and what life is like as your follower. Yokes and burdens are a part of life, Lord. I don't expect following you to be without responsibility. Help me not to be afraid. AMEN.

DAY 7: So then . . . Offer yourselves as a living sacrifice to God, dedicated to his service and pleasing to him. This is the true worship that you should offer. Do not conform yourselves to the standards of this world, but let God transform you inwardly by a complete change of your mind. Then you will be able to know the will of God—what is good and is pleasing to him and is perfect. ROMANS 12:1-2 TEV

PRAYER: Into my heart. Into my heart. Come into my heart, Lord Jesus. Come in today. Come in to stay. Come into my heart, Lord Jesus. AMEN.

BIBLIOGRAPHY

Bodner, Joan, ed. *Taking Charge of Our Lives: Living Responsibly in a Troubled World.* San Francisco: Harper & Row, 1984.

Boyer, Ernest, Jr. *Finding God at Home: Family Life As Spiritual Discipline.* San Francisco: Harper & Row, 1988.

Corson, Ben, Alice Tepper Marlin, Jonathan Schorsch, Anitra Swaminathan, and Rosalyn Will. *Shopping for a Better World: A Quick and Easy Guide to Socially Responsible Supermarket Shopping.* New York: Ballantine, 1989.

Crosby, O.F.M. and Michael H. Cap. *Spirituality of the Beatitudes: Matthew's Challenge for First World Christians.* New York: Orbis Books, 1981.

The Earth Works Group. *50 Simple Things You Can Do to Save the Earth.* Berkeley, Ca.: Earthworks Press, 1989.

Edwards, Tilden. *Living Simply Through the Day: Spiritual Survival in a Complex Age.* New York: Paulist Press, 1977.

Elgin, Duane. *Voluntary Simplicity: Toward a Way of Life That Is Outwardly Simple, Inwardly Rich.* New York: William Morrow, 1981.

Ewald, Ellen Buchman. *Recipes for a Small Planet.* New York: Ballantine, 1973.

Foster, Richard J. *Freedom of Simplicity.* San Francisco: Harper & Row, 1981.

Fox, Matthew. *A Spirituality Named Compassion and the Healing of the Global Village, Humpty Dumpty, and Us.* Minneapolis: Winston Press, 1979.

Kelsey, Morton T. *Adventure Inward: Christian Growth through Personal Journal Writing.* Minneapolis: Augsburg, 1980.

Johnson, Roberta Bishop, ed. *Whole Foods for the Whole Family: LaLeche League International Cookbook.* New York: New American Library, A Plume Book, 1981.

Leman, Dr. Kevin. *Bonkers: Why Women Get Stressed Out and What They Can Do About It.* Old Tappan, N.J.: Fleming H. Revell, 1987.

Longacre, Doris Janzen. *Living More with Less.* Scottdale, Pa.: Herald Press, 1980.

Longacre, Doris Janzen. *More-with-Less Cookbook.* Scottdale, Pa.: Herald Press, 1976.

May M.D., Gerald G. *Addiction and Grace.* San Francisco: Harper & Row, 1988.

Nouwen, Henri J. M. *Making All Things New: An Invitation to the Spiritual Life.* San Francisco: Harper & Row, 1981.

Schaef, Anne Wilson. *When Society Becomes an Addict.* San Francisco: Harper & Row, 1987.

Schramm, Mary R. *Extravagant Love: A Gospel Gift for Disarming the Heart.* Minneapolis: Augsburg, 1988.

Shames, Laurence. *The Hunger for More: Searching for Values in an Age of Greed.* New York: Times Books, 1989.

Simon, Arthur. *Bread for the World.* New York: Paulist Press, 1975.

Voran, Marilyn Helmuth. *Add Justice to Your Shopping List.* Scottdale, Pa.: Herald Press, 1986.

SOURCE NOTES

CHAPTER 2

Moving Down

1. Laurence Shames, *The Hunger for More: Searching for Values in an Age of Greed* (New York: New York Times Books, 1989), ix.
2. Harold J. Sutton, "Immortal Money: A Study of Tithing," *Alliance Witness* (March 17, 1965) 5.
3. Laurie Rubin, *Food First Curriculum* (San Francisco: Institute for Food and Development Policy, 1984), 14.

CHAPTER 3

Because I Can

1. Duane Elgin, *Voluntary Simplicity: Toward a Way of Life That Is Outwardly Simple, Inwardly Rich* (New York: William Morrow, 1981), 123.
2. Jorgen Lissner, Secretary for Peace, Justice and Human Rights, Lutheran World Federation, "Ten Reasons for Choosing a Simpler Life Style" (February 1983).
3. Ibid.

CHAPTER 4

Why Don't I Feel Good?

1. Robert Levine, "The Pace of Life," *Psychology Today* (October 1989), 44.
2. Ibid., 44, 46.

3. Ibid.
4. Connie Rose and Wesley Sime, "Stress and Immune Function in the Wellness Movement," *Wellness* (Summer 1987), 28.
5. Ibid.
6. *Psychology Today* (October 1989), 65-66.
7. Ibid., 66.

CHAPTER 6

Keeping the Main Thing the Main Thing

1. Kevin Leman, *Bonkers: Why Women Get Stressed Out and What They Can Do About It* (Old Tappan, N.J.: Fleming H. Revell, 1987), 188.
2. Richard J. Foster, *Freedom of Simplicity* (San Francisco: Harper & Row, 1981), 81.
3. Ibid., 89.
4. Joseph T. Plummer, "Changing Values," *The Futurist*, (January–February 1989), 8.

CHAPTER 7

A Call to Obedience

1. Duane Elgin, *Voluntary Simplicity: Toward a Way of Life That Is Outwardly Simple, Inwardly Rich* (New York: William Morrow, 1981), 96.
2. Ibid., 166.
3. Laurence Shames, *The Hunger for More*, 30.

CHAPTER 8

Half a Millennium in the Life of a Disposable Cup

1. *50 Simple Things You Can Do to Save the Earth*, (Berkeley, Ca.: The Earth Works Group, 1989).

CHAPTER 9

We Are What We Eat

1. Helen Bjornson, "Serving God in the Supermarket," *Lutheran Woman Today* (March 1990), 10-11.
2. Ibid., 11.

3. Marilyn Helmuth Voran, *Add Justice to Your Shopping List* (Scottdale, Pa.: Herald Press, 1986), 15-16.
4. Ibid., 16.
5. Ibid., 21.
6. Kevin Clarke, "Shopping with a Conscience Can Make You a Basket Case," *SALT* (January 1990), 6-12.
7. Ibid., 9.
8. Ibid., 21.
9. Arthur Simon, *Bread for the World* (New York: Paulist Press, 1975), 64.

CHAPTER 10

Come, Let Us Gather Together

1. Tilden Edwards, *Living Simply Through the Day: Spiritual Survival in a Complex Age* (New York: Paulist Press, 1977), 54.
2. Cover of quarterly devotional booklet from Order of Saints Martin and Teresa.
3. Ernest Boyer, Jr., *Finding God at Home: Family Life As Spiritual Discipline* (San Francisco: Harper & Row, 1988), 166-176.
4. Ibid., 173.
5. Ibid., 128.

CHAPTER 11

When I Feel Like a Failure

1. *Psychology Today*, (December 1989), 50.